On *Schoolhouse: Lessons on Love & Landscape*

"*Schoolhouse* offers the reader a wonderful journey as the immensely talented Marc Nieson explores the evolution of his younger self, a shy, brainy boy from the urban east coast, into a writer, an adult and an observer of the rural mid-west. He writes with bracing intelligence and the result is a memoir full of incidental wisdom and glittering moments—dissecting an owl pellet, watching the mist rise—that will stay with the reader long after the author reaches his destination. A wonderful debut."

—**Margot Livesey**, *Mercury*

"Marc Nieson's *Schoolhouse* is a record of wisdom and tenderness, and also a record of spiritual and emotional growth. Intelligent, wary, and observant, the narrator of this chronicle gradually lets us see into his heart and soul. It's a fine and wonderful book, beautifully written."

—**Charles Baxter**, *The Soul Thief* and *The Feast of Love*

"Those of us who have lived in old one-room schoolhouses understand the solitude, solace, and proximity to nature that they provide. During his year living in Union #9, Marc Nieson embraced these opportunities for inner growth. His new memoir—a must read—traces the story of his journey of discovery along the trail through the woods surrounding his house and along the path of human relationships. Read *Schoolhouse*, and you will open the door to the mind of an engaging voice, a probing, reflective writer who delights the reader with his lyrical prose on every page."

—**Mary Swander**, *Out of this World:*
A Woman's Life Among the Amish

"Toward the end of his memoir, Nieson says, 'We are all of us, to some extent, descendants of ice.' In this book, we begin to thaw."

—**Diane Glancy**, *Fort Marion Prisoners and the Trauma of Native Education* and *Report to the Department of the Interior*

"Marc Nieson's *Schoolhouse: Lessons on Love & Landscapes* is a thoughtful, engaging meditation on memory and place, fertile with striking and intimate detail of one man's early love affair and the lessons learned. A compelling story woven from whispered secrets, Nieson's book is a true gem of the memoir form."

—**Dinty W. Moore**, *Between Panic & Desire*

"*Schoolhouse* is an absolute joy, unquestionably one of the finest books to come out of the Midwest in years. Beautifully written, it's indeed a gift, a grateful giving back of what Nieson has discovered on his long and wonderful journey, and the lessons he teaches us are lessons we gladly carry forward."

—**Robert Hedin**, *At the Great Door of Morning*

"Years ago, I wrote: How does one paint a landscape of identity? Marc Nieson resoundingly answers that question in *Schoolhouse*, a remarkable memoir of love and landscape as well as a courageous narrative about writing and identity. One of the most poignant and beautiful memoirs I have read in decades…a collage of memories, place, and people…a memoir of fortitude and hope."

—**Marjorie Agosín**, *The White Islands* and
Of Earth And Sea: A Chilean Memoir

"There are life lessons aplenty in this gorgeous meditation on youth, love, and trying to find an anchor in the world. A book that should be widely read and appreciated for its insights and beauty, *Schoolhouse* utterly absorbed me in the lost world it creates and honors."

—**Robin Hemley**, *Nola: A Memoir of
Faith, Art, and Madness*

"The lyrical language of Marc Nieson's memoir is like the sound of memory itself. The wonderful prose transports the reader from Manhattan and Venice to the heartland of America in search of self and love in this movie of a memoir. I can't recommend this remarkable, moving memoir highly enough."

—**Chuck Kinder**, *Honeymooners: A Cautionary Tale*

"In this beautifully wrought memoir, Marc Nieson reclaims in spectacular detail a year he spent in a one-room country schoolhouse while attending the Iowa Writers' Workshop. It's a passionate recollection about how to get free of the loves that haunt us and won't let go, and how to keep at arm's length for a year, the clamoring world of New York City and Venice, Italy. Nieson find solace in the vibrant living natural world that surrounds his one-room Iowa schoolhouse. He mourns lost family members, and buries the dying animals that fall in the woods. By carefully recording the world around him, Nieson discovers his own authentic voice and a pathway out of the woods and back into the world. It's a lovely meditative of a stalled life rekindled by nature that harkens back to the finest work of Thoreau."

—**Joseph G. Peterson**, *Twilight of the Idiots*

"Marc Nieson knows full well how a lost relationship can both hurt and nourish one into being. In *Schoolhouse*, he has given us a remarkable book, light, grave, tender, unsettled, and wide, wide open to the mystery of letting go."

—**Paul Lisicky**, *The Narrow Door*

"A surprising page-turner of a memoir. Nieson comes to the Midwest with much baggage—Venice, a woman, New York—grappling to gain a better grip on his compass. I was both fascinated and informed anew by his heartland."

—**David Hamilton**, *Deep River: A Memoir of a Missouri Farm*

Schoolhouse

lessons on love & landscapes

Marc Nieson

*For Mary —
in ink + arms,*

Ice Cube Press
North Liberty, Iowa

Ice Cube Press, LLC (Est. 1993)
205 N. Front Street North Liberty, Iowa 52317
www.icecubepress.com steve@icecubepress.com
twitter: @icecubepress

Assisting Project Editor: Adam Jaschen

Cover design: Jane Farthing, www.2farthings.com

Cover schoolhouse photos: Marc Nieson

Grateful acknowledgments to the following publications for originally printing excerpts from this book, some differently titled or in slightly different form: *The Literary Review*: "What I Did on My Summer Vacation," *The Iowa Review*: "Every December," *Green Mountains Review*: "In the Basement," *Chautauqua*: "Lessons in Anatomy," *Prairie Gold: An Anthology of the American Heartland* (Ice Cube Press): "Lost and Found," *Lime Hawk*: "Music Appreciation," *TriQuarterly* (a publication of Northwestern University): "Orientation."

For James Alan McPherson
teacher & compass

Only that day dawns to which we are awake.

—H. D. Thoreau

*And the day came when the risk to remain tight in a bud
was more painful than the risk it took to blossom.*

—Anaïs Nin

Lesson Plan

❧

Pre-School 1

Orientation 5

Geography 15

Civics 34

Spelling 46

Reading 65

Anatomy 90

History 117

Homework 139

Social Studies 160

Music Appreciation 179

Lost & Found 191

Weights & Measures 207

What I Did On My
Summer Vacation 224

Commencement 250

Acknowledgments 259

Pre-School

Sometimes it is like a dream. A sleepwalking. The way you move through your surroundings—through doorways, backyards, decades—one unconscious foot following the other. Perhaps for a moment you're able to focus on a color or sound or even a face, yet before you can name it, it passes.

Or sometimes, it may just be a memory unblurring before you. A day in 1992 for example. Early autumn, as I recall: I am standing on my head atop a hillside somewhere in the midst of the Midwest, and I am not dreaming. What I am doing is trying to make an ocean out of the endless sky, trying to link this landscape with another I can at least recognize. My bare toes dangle into the froth of clouds below and soon a pair of hawks floats by, belly-up, revealing white underwings. A faint fluttering rises within my chest. The wingbeats of memory? A fading photograph? A woman's name—Sybil.

I dig my brow into the grass for a better hold, but soon grow dizzy and drop my feet back to the ground. Thankfully my shadow is still there, slanting below. What with the earth spinning at over a thousand miles per hour, both balance and bearings seem critical.

Most of us are thrust into this world headfirst and upside down. Most, quickly slapped into our first awareness. They tell me the doctor struck three times before I cried out, for which I was dubbed stubborn. Of course I can't remember the incident, but have always figured I was just a little stunned for the moment at the sudden light. Waiting for focus. For a clarity to sink in.

It took until grade school before a reading teacher recognized I was actually myopic. Each year a thicker pair of eyeglasses helped better frame the blackboard's many lessons, and by the end of high school contact lenses added some peripheries, but the truth is the bigger picture kept escaping me. I remained shortsighted and slow to respond to what passed before me. Slow to get things said or done, playing catch up for much of my life.

Stumbling toward hindsight, I've come to call it.

❧

And now, somehow the year is 2016 and the place Pittsburgh, wherein I find myself a fifty-five year-old man. I'm standing more upright this time, and have since had cataract surgery. I wake up to a world that's strangely in focus each morning. I'm happily married near on twenty years, and together we've raised a bold and beautiful daughter who'll be heading off to college any day now. And so, I also wake up most mornings feeling pretty lucky and thankful. Feeling quite distant from the younger man who used to live alone and so squinty-eyed on that remote Midwestern hillside.

So then, why bother returning? Why bother rehashing the past at all? Why revisit that particular place, that single year when everything in my little life turned upside down? If you were to visit that Iowa hilltop today, you'd find the ground similarly overgrown with wildflowers and weeds, but if you looked closer you might notice a slight dent underfoot, suggesting what was a foundation to a small square building. So part of my reason has to do with what once stood there and deserves due homage. And part resides with what has remained sunken somewhere in the middle of my chest ever since. Call it matters of the heart, or of the heartland, if you will.

I've come to think we all experience one love that stays with us, at least one impassioned relationship that, for better or worse, upends us. For me, mine just happened to be a May-December affair. When it started, I was barely twenty-one, and Sybil turning forty. Me, a babe in the woods of Manhattan's skyscrapers, and she already married and separated, a mother of three boys the eldest of whom was merely three years younger than me. Ridiculous? Perhaps. Fabulous and deluded, fated to fail? For sure. And yet we went on together for ten years.

And decades later, while all those years are well in my rearview, some nights she still turns up in my dreams, wandering in unresolved. Clearly, something finally and fully needed to be addressed. Or better yet, redressed, for the way we both did and didn't part ways.

So maybe instead of a recounting, let's call what follows an accounting. An attempt to finally put an old throbbing to rest. A textbook of lessons I wish I'd already been schooled in at the time. A study guide for the incurable romantics among us all. Or, call it an elegy for a hilltop, an homage to what once was. A cautionary tale regarding what may or may not be sustainable in love and landscapes. What might still be turned aright. What should never go left unsaid, undone.

Orientation

I remember Sybil was wearing a yellow-green jumpsuit on the night we first met, its material parachute-like in both sheen and movement. Remember how its fabric made a certain whispering sound as she shifted in her seat in the row before me. At the time we were sitting in an auditorium at The New School, two strangers among an audience of two hundred attending an evening Adult-Ed film course. Late Spring of 1981.

And of course I recall noticing her hair, too—its forest of tameless black curls partly pulled back by a large plastic clip. Her neck thus lay partially exposed, revealing an olive complexion that played off her yellow collar nicely. So yes, I was sneaking glances. Sidelong glimpses of her petite profile, one sculpted cheekbone, her glossed twin lips. At that moment, however, we were still just two orbiting souls, unaware of the improbable synchronicity that makes any chance coupling occur.

As it turns out, that evening was the last class of the semester, and the two of us wound up among a handful of fellow students milling about the stage's proscenium. The professor was taking down names of potential volunteers for the following Fall, as he needed several ushers and ticket takers. The course was charismatic for its day, involving previewed screenings of feature films a week before they opened followed by live interviews with a secret guest—the film's director or cinematographer or a surprise celebrity from its cast. A class that drew eager enrollment from the neighboring Tri-State area, not so much "returning" students as curious suburban housewives with their commuting husbands, what were called the "bridge and tunnel" crowd by the more seasoned Upper Westsiders seated beside them. In short, a houseful of mostly middle-aged, middle-class movie lovers.

So, what was I doing there? Floundering, I suspect. At twenty-one I'd already dropped out of Business School and was blundering through a series of dead-end jobs. And I'll admit, at the time I too was living out in the heart of Long Island's suburbia, with my parents no less. But I was flirting with the idea of film school in the big city. With moving into Manhattan!

As for why Sybil was there, I can't say. She didn't look middle-aged and, as I would soon learn, was part Portuguese, part black Irish, and lived in Spanish Harlem. Certainly she was no demure housewife. So I'm fairly certain it must have been she who spoke first, who broke the ice between us, because I wasn't only painfully young but painfully shy. Not only still a virgin at twenty-one, but someone who'd never even kissed a girl yet.

But that evening I must have been bolder than usual. Perhaps I overheard her name pronounced to the professor and thought, *Now there's an intriguing name to go along with that exotic jumpsuit.* Or perhaps it was Sybil who suggested we get a coffee. In any event, I do recall recommending the Kiev, an all-night Ukrainian restaurant over on 2nd Avenue I knew would be open. In fact, I don't think they even had a key for its front door.

Considering the marquee brilliance of what that evening came to ignite in my life, it's no surprise it all began among the closing credits of a movie class. In memory's archives, the scene plays out like a montage of images: our walking over to the Eastside together; the crowded sidewalks along St. Mark's Place; Sybil's flat white shoes, all scuffed and sole thin; and how quickly she walked for someone her height; how quickly she talked. Yes, there was an electricity to Sybil. A halo of curiosity, a palpable vibration in the air surrounding her that felt as exciting and immediate as the silver screen.

Once inside the Kiev, we hid any initial awkwardness behind our menus. I could hardly sit still, let alone keep myself from stealing peeks at her downturned gaze, her eyelashes, her perfect chin. Was she real, this moment really happening? The waitress arrived and Sybil chose their classic mushroom barley soup. Finally blinking, I ordered the eggs and kasha. Within the minute, cups of coffee and buttered challah were set before us. Two slices each.

"This bread is incredible," she said. "Do you think we can get more?"

I watched her eat with tapered fingers, her fawn eyes reflecting the overhead fluorescents. Already I was infatuated.

"So, you think we'll get to be on staff next semester?" I said.

"Hope so. Free classes then. And movies!"

It had been a banner season for premieres. *Chariots of Fire* and *My Dinner with Andre*. *Prince of the City* and *On Golden Pond*. *Reds, Diva, Gallipoli*. And two with Paul Newman—*Fort Apache* and *Absence of Malice*.

"His interview was the best one, don't you think?"

"Hands down," said Sybil.

"You know I bumped into him in the men's room."

"You didn't."

"No, really. And his eyes, up close? You wouldn't believe."

I could've been talking about hers.

"Cerulean?" she said.

"Huh? Yeah, that'd be the word. Or drop-dead would do."

She smiled at me, strangely. My eyes were blue too, but nothing like Newman's. Not even as sultry as Treat Williams'.

"You're not gay, are you?" she asked.

I set down my coffee cup. "No. Do I look it?"

"No, nor do you act it. It's just, nice I guess…to hear a young man be able to appreciate another man's beauty. Must be your generation."

The waitress brought our orders and we dug in, as pleased for the food as the distraction. No doubt Sybil was more aware of my youth than I was at guessing her age. Still, the moment felt a little weird. Again, like something out of a movie. *Summer of '42. The Graduate.* And while no overt seducing was going on at our table, there were no pretensions of innocence either. Our semester had run rife with other premieres, too—*Body Heat* and *The Postman Always Rings Twice, The French Lieutenant's Woman, Lady Chatterly's Lover.*

All I knew was here was this stunning woman suddenly sitting before me like some starlet, embodying all the energy and urgency of the city itself. Radiating the very neon intensity I knew I'd been lacking in my life to date. Right there, an arm's length away. I'd never felt a yearning like that before.

And what felt even more surprising: across the table I could sense her attraction, too. No woman, or girl for that matter, had ever shown any interest in me before. Or at least none I'd been aware of. What flickered for Sybil that evening, I can only guess—the fresh attentions of a young buck as balm for her broken marriage? A brief summer romance, a fling? One thing for certain, the connection between us was definitely running parallel, the pull undeniable.

Because later, before we parted on the subway, Sybil handed me her card, on which she'd quickly scribbled her home phone number—something she admitted she never did. I remember glancing down at her handwriting, all felt-tipped and florid, hovering over some graphic logo. At the restaurant she'd mentioned one of her jobs was as a detailing rep for a pharmaceutical company. What I remember most, however, is how right before I stepped off the train and she continued uptown, she quickly kissed me. And right on the lips.

All right, let's add entranced to my feeling infatuated. Smitten, maybe even a little bit drugged. I stepped off onto the bleary platform and turned—the idling subway's doors still open, her strange and enchanting taste on my lips, the memory of how she'd shrugged when I caught her wrapping what was left of her challah in a napkin and stuffing it into her shoulder bag.

As the train pulled away, through its window I saw her smiling to herself in a private moment—a touch embarrassed, a touch sad, a touch hopeful—and I recognized we were more than just passing trains in the night. It was as if we were destined to meet, to save one another.

And so our affair began. Under the umbrella of movies, mushroom barley, and romance. We stumbled through that first summer, meeting up at museums and theaters, tentatively pawing at one another on park benches like teenagers. I lost my virginity one night in Central Park, on a hillside opposite the Alice in Wonderland statue, Sybil giggling in the faint glow of a streetlight. This is crazy, I thought. Surreal. Splendid.

Soon, though, September came knocking. Motivated by the growing chill outdoors, I found myself a tiny rent-stabilized apartment near the bottom of Lexington Avenue. Each Friday I'd buy Sybil a bouquet of flowers and pull out the arts section of the *New York Times* to select which new films or gallery openings or dance concerts to attend that weekend. Back then theatre tickets weren't yet so prohibitive, and the fashions of Norma Kamali and Issey Miyake free to study in shopfront windows. Through Sybil I was discovering not only the big city's avenues and art, but what true beauty could be, what felt alive and enduring. I was even catching glimpses of myself in her eyes. What I might have to offer a person, a culture.

Our first dizzying year passed like this, and then another. Sybil would stay over at my apartment one or two nights per week yet always leave come morning, and I never entered her Spanish Harlem home. None of this was ever spoken about, just understood. If the arrangement was odd, I didn't know it. Again, this was the first relationship I'd ever had. In large part I followed her lead, tickled by whatever time and love we could share. We hardly socialized with anyone else, our rapport remaining more tryst-like and in the present moment. Freed from the banalities of bills and laundry, the complexities of future tense.

Deep down I was probably as confused as ever, but seemingly more confident, focused. I enrolled in NYU's film school and managed to complete a BFA, but then promptly went back to another myopic string of odd jobs. Months and years were ticking by during which I checked off fleeting flirtations with construction work, bicycle messengering, theater box offices, two stints abroad in Italy teaching ESL, even a season with a one-ring circus—in all, a virtual diploma's worth of detours and detachments.

The only real attachment I could claim, the sole vocation I'd been able to commit myself to and sustain whole-heartedly, was Sybil. Through it all, we remained an item, and I default to so generic and undefined a word because I don't know precisely what else to call us. Loyal? Yes, yet you couldn't say we were "going out," let alone going forward. We weren't boyfriend-girlfriend or budding fiancés, cuckolds or adulterers. Frankly there was and remains no socially recognized word for what we were. The closest construct at the time may have been an old gay couple—unable to live entirely together or apart. Coming and going, yet always coming back to each other. Mutual harbors, across town or across the ocean, for better and worse, for ten years and counting. Sybil, my prophetess and soothsayer. Part sylph and symphony. Music and muse. Hearth and island. Whatever you might choose to call her or us, to date, Sybil was surely the closest I'd ever come to a lodestar in my life.

And yet now I was taking off again, trying out yet another potential vocation. This time my plan was to attend graduate school, which seemed levelheaded enough. While filmmaking hadn't necessarily agreed with me, writing did. I felt like I needed to pursue that passion. Maybe even move on to what was next for me.

So, come one humid morning in late summer, Sybil and I found ourselves standing opposite one another on a lower Lexington Avenue sidewalk. At the curbside sat my car, its trunk wedged full, my apartment upstairs sublet for now. She handed me my last bag, which I slid across the front seat. I turned back, noting her slender face flanked by one of the many pairs of dangling earrings I'd given her over the years. Sybil could pull off any sized earring.

"So," she said, the both of us now empty-handed.

I could feel sweat running under my arms. See a similar drop pooling in the tiny dint between Sybil's collarbones. I reached out and dampened it with my fingertip.

I glanced away at the passing traffic. At the courses of brick on the building across the street. At our feet, where a tiny yellow candy wrapper lay on the curb. Anywhere, but into her eyes.

"So," I started, but it was all I too could muster.

We stood on for another moment or two, then reached out for our hug and kiss goodbye.

Was this what a decade together was all coming down to? Some scrap of litter on the sidewalk and an awkward embrace? How could I be leaving her at that curbside? How could I *ever* leave Sybil behind?

Still, I felt the jolt of the car slipping into gear below me. Saw the back of her dress receding in the rearview mirror. Midway through the Holland Tunnel I started to hyperventilate, the dashboard swimming.

Wait, where are you flitting to now? Iowa?! God, you must really be crazy this time. Turn around, turn back.

Yet I didn't. Couldn't, not anymore. One of us had to take a step, even if that step was one of retreat. Even if neither of us could admit that's what was happening.

Geography

Hundreds of miles passed before my vision cleared. The blurred swath of asphalt ahead turned into lanes and eventually I noticed a copse of trees beyond the road's shoulder, a sign mentioning Ohio. I veered off the interstate, steering the car toward more open land, sifting through small towns with alluring names like Defiance and Peru. Night fell and the odometer kept spinning. The windshield clouded over with dead flies, the radio drowning in static, but as long as I kept moving, everything was okay.

At some point I must've pulled over, exhausted, because the next thing I recall was waking up sprawled in the backseat. The rising sun was already streaming in, the windows open wide, the Illinois state line flitting somewhere in the back of my head. And, I swear, the near field's rustle of cornstalks whispering, *Sybil, Sybil, Sybil.*

What was I doing out here?

I gassed up the car, grabbed a coffee, and pointed the Pontiac further west. Soon a decent song blossomed from the radio, and with each passing farmstead I could feel a gradual unfurling within me. With each passing mile, the horizon grew more rolling and manicured, the air thick with promise. Finally I crossed the Mississippi River at the very spot Joliet and Marquette first documented three hundred years earlier. On the other side of the bridge stood a shiny road sign reading *"IOWA: A Place to Grow."*

I smiled, the first in days. Probably weeks. Maybe this wasn't so far-fetched after all, I thought. Outside my window, row after row of cropland was whizzing by, strobe-like and hypnotic, lush. I took a deep breath and right there and then made a vow to live in the country. To really try to start a new life in a new landscape. Apart and alone.

I spent my first week in Iowa City bedding down in the car. A public park curved alongside the river on the north edge of town with dirt parking lots and an umbrella of tree branches— as of yet the closest I'd ever come to camping. I'd wake up feeling equally refreshed and foolish, then grab a fistful of quarters to telephone real estate agents at the nearest phone booth. Stubborn, maybe, but I was holding out for anything but another apartment.

Once the local Yellow Pages were exhausted, I thumbed through circulars outside supermarkets, scoured bulletin boards at neighborhood laundromats, the public library. Surely locating a country farmhouse to rent couldn't be as hard as scoring a cheap efficiency in Manhattan. In the past, my modus operandi always lay in patience. After all, in New York City whatever you needed eventually bumped into you on the street. For better or worse, I'd long believed all good things come to those who wait.

In Iowa, this didn't seem to be working.

So I started driving the rural roads myself, knocking on doors. Folks were kind enough, but every last one stared at me slightly askance. Maybe it was my accent or dark urban clothes. Or maybe just my ponytail. Whichever, clearly I was standing on their porches uninvited and unschooled in how things were done out here. What few leads I did receive all led back to my car.

Come nightfall I'd return to the city park, dusty and dejected. Happy couples strolled by arm-in-arm, some with small children grasping ice cream cones and skipping toward the kiddie rides. I'd sit on a park bench and watch the spinning carousel until all the lights turned out, then crawl into my car and lay my head onto its bare upholstery. One night I fell asleep outdoors, in the rocking arms of the Ferris wheel. On paper that may sound romantic, but trust me, it wasn't. Dreaming of Sybil and sneaking morning shaves at a Sinclair gas station. Showering at the public pool. Driving halfway across the country to be homeless and hungry and alone. Pitiful. But goddamn it, if I'd come to the Midwest I was going to live in the corn. I was going to grow, just like that sign said.

Finally I spoke with a bank manager who said he knew of a homestead outside a nearby town called Lone Tree. I liked the sound of that, and drove the twenty-five miles (nearby?) to find a solitary, two-story farmhouse. Its surface was weathered grey, its window shades brittle and half drawn, and out back grew eighty standing acres of corn. Perfect, I thought, the very image. Who cares if it wasn't available for another two months. I had my car and the city park, my choice of parking spots. I could wait, I told myself.

As I drove back toward Iowa City the surrounding fields literally shimmered in the late afternoon light. In my rearview mirror rose a long tail of gravel dust, like some smoke screen for all the doubts that lay behind me. I pulled over and climbed onto the car's roof, trying to glimpse the end of the corn. My shadow stretched out onto the stalks and I waved at my silhouette, standing just as tall and patient among them. Yes, I could do this, I thought. Find my roots out here in the open, plow myself a whole new path.

Back at the city park that night, however, I fell asleep with the dashboard radio on and woke up to a dead battery. The surrounding parking lot stretched empty and silent, save for a couple of crows mocking me from a near treetop. I paced and cursed and kicked at the gravel, then fetched a pair of pliers from the glove box and managed to loosen the battery terminals.

"Don't I know you from somewhere?" asked the attendant at the Sinclair station.

I lifted the battery onto his countertop and averted my eyes.

"No," I said, "I just moved here."

"You sure?"

I was nearly out of breath from the walk.

"Yeah," I said, "I'm from New York."

He shook his head and pulled the battery toward him. "New York City?"

"Yes," I said. "New York City."

"I could swear I've seen you somewhere— "

"Look, can you charge this up or what?"

The walk back to the car felt even longer, the battery heavier, and by then, of course, it had started to rain. One of those flash summer storms, sudden and unforgiving. With each plodding step, Lone Tree seemed an eternity away. Finally reaching the city park's entrance, I stood there soaking wet and tried to picture myself hiding out for another sixty nights, rolling over in my sleep as the chill of autumn pressed in through the car doors. Who was I kidding?

That afternoon, I took a share in an old duplex in town. A humble Civil War era home with a deep porcelain sink in the kitchen and a porch swing out front—offering tons more room than my tiny NYC efficiency, but decidedly NOT rural. I unloaded the Pontiac's trunk and settled in as best I could, because within a couple of weeks classes were starting up at the university. At the Writers' Workshop.

At thirty-one years old it felt thrilling to sit in a classroom again, and not any classroom, but one filled with a dozen other comrades all hell-bent on learning how to write a good story. Among them, for perhaps the first time in my life, I didn't need to explain myself or apologize for wanting to construct fictions. Perhaps I'd finally found my fellow tribe, a territory where I might finally belong.

Despite being one of the older students, I almost immediately felt intimidated. In seminar classes it grew painfully obvious how well-educated and versed my classmates were in the landscape and language of literature and criticism. I sensed how poorly read I was, how sporadically I'd managed to educate myself. All I knew was that I adored well-told stories and felt at home sitting alone in a room for hours on end making things up in my head.

Thankfully, the academic demands on us proved minimal. The Writers' Workshop's main focus was on mentorship and giving us unhindered time at our desks to practice our craft and diligence. I'd have the chance to write and read and get myself up to speed, not to mention personal access to Pulitzer prize-winning professors. In our "workshop" classes—wherein we mutually critiqued each other's works-in-progress—it also became evident how all that background in literary theory didn't necessarily insure you could render a good tale of your own on the page. At least not yet. At the drafting desk, we were all apprentices.

So mostly I stayed to myself, trying to fill pages with fresh words, tooling around with make-believe characters in conflict. Each week we'd all meet for workshop class around a big table like a family sitting down to break bread together. I felt incredibly fortunate and sated, and before long looked up to note the first autumn semester had flown by. All along, Sybil and I kept in intermittent contact, writing letters or dialing one another on the phone late at night. But as winter came the nights grew longer and the snow deep, the physical distance between us proving harder to endure. Come spring break, she came to Iowa for a visit.

I recall it feeling awkward at first. I didn't quite know how to introduce her to my new friends, and our rhythms felt off among company. In Iowa I was engaging in a much wider social life, if slower than the one we'd shared in New York City. Downtown Iowa City was barely a few square blocks with but one movie house, a place where one's clothes and personal style weren't the common currency either. No doubt Sybil felt removed from this new life of mine, if not a touch threatened. Just as in New York there always existed a part of her domestic life from which I duly remained separate. In Iowa, our unspoken contract felt strangely public. Our modus operandi, suddenly questionable.

Compartmentalizing your life in a city as big as New York wasn't all too unusual a practice—perhaps a necessary evil, even a survival skill. For the most part, no one there questioned who was on your arm, and no one nosed into your business because they were all too busy keeping pace with their own. But on a small Midwestern sidewalk, Sybil and I may well have looked suspect. Certainly with the studied style and aura she evoked. Plus, we couldn't just retreat since I had a roommate in my Iowa City duplex.

As a consequence, Sybil and I repaired north to a bigger city. Neither of us had ever been to Minneapolis, and so we took a drive. This too wasn't all that unusual for us. Over the years we'd taken many trips together, both in the US and abroad. We traveled extremely well together, equally curious and drawn to explore new museums and galleries, theaters and restaurants—not unlike how we shared time back in Manhattan. In Minneapolis, we did the same—visiting The Walker and The Guthrie, trying out Uptown cafés and holing up in our motel room. As always, we relished one another's affections and appetites, intoxicated by our bodies' familiar sense of intimacy and exile. Our easy give and take. Our time together, unnamed. Present. Same as it ever was.

Driving back to Iowa, however, popped that bubble. Our long and lush weekend swiftly shrunk away into the rearview mirror. Minnesota's rural backroads were lovely, the flanking fields and trees starting to show their first verdant blush, but increasingly I found myself focusing on the passing silos and silence. I reached across the seat for Sybil's hand, clutching at what neither of us could admit loomed ahead on the horizon.

At the Cedar Rapids airport, I saw her off at the gate. We stood there as long as we could.

"This is starting to become a habit," she said.

"Yeah." And a bad one, I thought, but of course said nothing further.

I hugged her close then sat in the parking lot crying. The dashboard before me, once again swimming. Nearby a farmer chugged by on his John Deere planter, devotedly seeding a harrowed ocean of land. I felt all aimless and awash again. Ungrounded. Confounded.

Come summer, I didn't return to New York. I stayed in Iowa City writing, and right before my second year at the university started, an untilled tract of land presented itself to me. Fifteen miles west of Iowa City winds a road listed on maps as F52. Locally, they call it Black Diamond Road, and geographically it bisects farmland between the Amana Colonies and Kalona's Amish, attending a creek they call Old Man. The creek, however, doesn't entirely listen to the road and at one point branches off to the north. In the cradle of land between those waters lies a floodplain and several wooded ridges; rare acreage that has somehow managed to elude both ax and plow. And on the crest of one of those ridges, behind a windbreak of tall pine, stands an old one-room schoolhouse.

Or, at least, it once stood there.

At the time, however, those were pretty much the directions I received from the owner over the phone. Other roads intersected with names like Half Moon and Hazelwood, but they weren't mentioned. Nor were any addresses. Simply: follow Black Diamond past the second creek crossing, turn right at the mailbox marked Redbird Farm, and bear left up the hill. Oh, and know the gate might be closed if the drive is too muddy.

Driving southwest out of Iowa City, the traffic lights gradually gave way to open fields. It had been exactly a year since my initial drive west from New York, and once again I was hesitantly considering a move—yet feeling hopeful about this new lead, this projected image of some romantic rural life still awaiting me. I veered onto Black Diamond Road, its sparkling two lanes lazily curving past old farmsteads of sheep and pigs, pasture and crop. Once the road straightened, I could see a small green bridge marking the second creek ahead. Beyond that stood a mailbox, stenciled with two little brown and white birds on a branch. I rechecked the scribbled directions in my lap—*Redbird* Farm?

I pulled off the road and parked before the chained gate. The drive beyond indeed looked wet and spongy. I hopped up onto the gate's middle rung to better scan the area. Clumps of overgrown grass half-camouflaged a grey barn nearby, and an old white house sat nestled among willows across the road, but no schoolhouse in sight. I started climbing over the gate but my pants' leg caught on an exposed nail, and before I knew it I was flailing in mid-air, then ankle-deep in muck.

Normally I would've laughed it off, just another clumsy lurch in an ongoing resume of missteps. Yet gazing down at my sorry mud-caked self, I started to question my greater balance again. What was I *really* doing out here, and not just looking for a schoolhouse but coming to Iowa in the first place? What the *hell* was I thinking? Trading Manhattan and Sybil, for this mud heap? And for what, to study fiction writing? Come on, get real. What the hell was I *doing* with my life?

I trudged uphill, head down, doubt mounting with each mired footstep. My whole life slowly bubbled up for review. Every false or stalled start. All my veering detours and varied pit stops. Transition after transition after transition. Face it, there was no plan going on here. There was no plan whatsoever. It was all just one more muddy, muddled mess I'd have to dig myself out of. Stumbling toward hindsight, I thought. Once again, stumbling toward hindsight.

Then, I noticed the drive beneath me was drying out, the ground leveling. I looked up and there before me squatted a small, old-time schoolhouse—rising out of the hilltop, square and assured. Its clapboard was the color of worn work shoes and a green ivy swept up its stone chimney, a lightning rod climbing higher still at mid-roof, bearing a tiny glass globe as milky blue as the sky. And all around flowed a staggering expanse of rolling meadows and woodland, a flickering green carpet of cornstalks on the far horizons. Acre after acre, miles of perspective.

I felt the breath lodge in my throat, my knees nearly buckling in disbelief. The ground beneath me was solid, though. I was standing on solid ground.

Within the week I repacked my Pontiac and moved in. The schoolhouse's interior proved as spare and intimate as its backyard was majestic and enticing. A mere twenty-five by twenty-five feet, you'd think it was a step back toward apartment living for me, but the ceiling vaulted a full dozen feet overhead, and a loft area added another third of living space where I situated my writing desk and bed. A good half of the building's four walls were girded in glass, each window tall and wide, mullioned and bright. I counted seventeen in all, over sixty gridded panes!

Back in New York my teeny apartment had but two windows: one in the bathroom opaque, the other yielding no more than forty minutes of sun per day. Or secondhand sun, I should say, since even that came reflecting off someone else's window down the alley. And my apartment's lone view faced a solid brick wall, beyond bolted security gates.

So added to the schoolhouse's overwhelming generosity of space and light came its atmosphere of liberation. The outdoors felt inside, and the inside out. On my first morning, I threw back the bed sheets, scrambled down the loft's ladder, and stood naked before the largest span of windows. Roll call was brief, being I was the only one in attendance. No, wait. In the far pasture grazed several horses with necks bent and tails swishing. Dew clung to the flowering grasses nearby, and warm shadows beckoned from the closest stand of trees. My new neighbors, I thought, my classmates. I ought to learn all their names.

I bounded out the door onto the schoolhouse's wooden deck, the morning air tingling my skin. I leapt up onto the railing then promptly urinated out over the edge. Instinctively marking my territory, I guess. Certainly couldn't do that off my fire escape in Manhattan.

"Present," I shouted aloud.

After a moment, my voice returned from the opposite ridge. "Present!"

From that very first morning, I figured if I intended to recalibrate *how* to be in this new world, then I should probably start with *where* I now was in that landscape. I'd begin then, with a map. This might seem the obvious choice, but wandering and adapting had always been my more natural impulses, not to mention quite handy for never having to explain where I was going or from where I'd come. Traits, I guessed, which were part inherited.

My bloodline, or at least those few who managed to escape Poland before the Second World War, came to New York seeking shelter. The men all lived and worked indoors—one grandfather in a kosher butcher shop, the other a hat factory, and later my father in various engineering plants. The same held true for the women. My mother took steno and plucked typewriter keys under office fluorescence, not unlike her mother who'd plucked chickens and then their lice from her forearms. My other grandmother had been mostly blind, which restricted her to a two-room tenement that smelled of mothballs. I came from a place where land was based on asphalt and numbered avenues, not open acreage. Where trees were confined to the reservations of square city parks and even then hard to find—from Brooklyn. A place where I'd learned nature wasn't something you tried to embrace, but avoid. Even your own nature.

However, here on a quiet Iowa hillside, I was hoping to change all that. To both learn and unlearn who I was. To try living not only alone and apart, but a more consciously observed life—both inside and out.

Toward that end, I bought myself a new notebook to begin a journal. I chose one of those black and white speckled composition books, which seemed apt for the schoolhouse. On its first page I drew a small square, marked an X within to stand for the building's pitched roof, then made another concentric square for its wrap-around wooden deck. I hesitated, then in block letters wrote, "**YOU ARE HERE.**"

At the far left base of the schoolhouse's hill lay a small pond, beyond which a thin trail led into the near woods. Seated on the schoolhouse's porch, I sketched these details into my journal then slipped it underarm and strode downhill like some wide-eyed tourist.

Mere minutes into the brush I came upon blackberries. Hundreds upon hundreds of them, arching out from laden brambles along the trail. Some still red and turning, others overripe and practically bursting their shiny skin. At the barest nudge of fingertips they'd plop off into my palm. Tart or sweet, I swallowed them all, mouthful after mouthful. I imagined this is what it must have felt like to go camping as a kid, or to grow your own food. It sure beat the crowded produce aisle at D'Agostino in Manhattan. The only swarms here were tiny mosquitoes, who seemed equally eager to feed on my forearms. I stuffed my cheeks one last time and trotted off.

The next bend in the trail revealed a second pond. A fine mist clung to its surface like smoke, curling into the shadows of old oaks crowding the banks. The smells seemed more pungent there, earthen and unfamiliar. I cracked open my notebook and sketched the basin's contours, larger and more irregular than the first pond's oval. At its edge spread a skirt of green algae, here and there pocked by sunken branches. And look, frogs! Nearly everywhere I glanced brought a surprise. Further along the bank lay an overturned rowboat. Whoever's it was wouldn't mind, would they?

Once freed from the undergrowth, the boat slid easily into the pond. All was hush save for my clumsy dipping of oars, which snagged on trains of algae near the banks. Gaining deeper water, I turned the boat about, stern forward, and rowed a mock Venetian style to better see where I was going— something I'd learned while living in Italy a few years prior. In retrospect, Venice too was a place I'd moved to based on not much more than an intuition.

Back while attending NYU, I worked a midnight shift backing up data tapes for an air travel discounter in midtown. As a perk I got two free flights to Europe, so Sybil and I flew to Amsterdam then hurtled from Scandinavia to Greece on a three-week Eurail pass. With a breathless indulgence we imbibed as many great cities' museums and fare as we could, and with only two days left ferried back from Athens to Brindisi where one train was heading to Rome in four hours, another to Venice in forty minutes. And so we ran.

In short, the maze and mystique of Venice's alleyways spun my head quicker than *prosecco*. Sybil and I were in the city barely an afternoon before having to hop an overnight train to Zurich for our flight home, but I immediately knew I needed to return and reside in Venice. Among its curving canals and dead end alleyways, its slow and shifting tides, I recognized my reflection. Here was a place where maps proved utterly useless, where being dizzy and lost felt like the natural order. In fact, I sensed losing one's bearings in Venice was half its grace. The city itself part chimera, drifting somewhere between sea and sky, moored not so much to land or time as the imagination. A world afloat.

Once upon a time I'd dreamed of setting foot in every zip code across America, of spending six months in every country on every continent. In this way I'd gradually map out the globe with my feet, which in my mid-twenties still didn't seem so farfetched. Come early spring of 1987 I set course for Venice, this time without Sybil on what I decided would be the first leg of my proposed world tour. I found part-time work with an English language institute, stayed three months then returned to New York, ostensibly for a friend's wedding. By autumn I was back in Italy, so suited to Venice's rhythms and remove I didn't feel the need to explore anywhere else.

If only calendars could have been similarly ignored. That second year I learned touring abroad and living abroad were entirely different matters. Certainly, living apart from Sybil. While she came to Venice for two short sumptuous visits, and I commuted back to New York to avoid Italy's summer tourist season, the nights and months away grew increasingly painful.

Sometime during my third year in Venice, I recognized I could only venture so far or long away from her. It occurred to me that maybe I hadn't come to Italy to embark on some purported world tour, but—at least subconsciously—to see if I *could* distance myself from Sybil. The sudden chill of that realization rifled through my body and I spent the next several days in bed with a high fever. A stomach virus followed, and over the next month I shed over thirty pounds. They melted right off me whether I ate or not, the bones in my cheeks and ribcage casting shadows. In the mirror, I literally scared myself—so much so, I soon flew back to New York like some helplessly migrating bird, pulled as much by my desire for Sybil as by my dismay of possibly losing her.

Once back in the same city, it became obvious that our rapport, our entanglement, was at least in part addictive. We tried going cold turkey, but proximity now made it even more impossible to resist. Sybil would turn up at the circus box office where I was working, and I'd duly backflip with DTs. Anxiety attacks ensued, and handfuls of hair started falling out of my head.

From out of that mania arose the idea of applying to graduate school in Iowa, a sort of halfway house—distant enough, if still in the same hemisphere. A place where I might be able to retreat and reboot. A place where she might feel less pulled to visit. Where we *both* might stand half a chance of not relapsing.

And so there I was, in an Iowa rowboat a thousand miles away from Spanish Harlem, listening to the creak of oarlocks below me. What reared up, however, was the feel of those old Venetian canals sliding below me. That loose and lazy meandering through my days that marked my last time away from New York. No, I thought, you can't go on with that way of life anymore. Eyes wide open and conscious now. I had to be more aware and methodical, had to make sure this voyage would be different from that cobblestone maze in Venice, from that unresolved curbside on Lexington Avenue.

8 August '92. Evening. 8:30 PM. Noticing this journal requires not only dates, but also times. A kind of map to cover temporal coordinates, too? The landscape constantly changing with the light, shifting within a moment's breath.

> *the span of a wing beat*
> *a falling petal*
> *a footstep*

Are there specific hours when these deer emerge from the lower pasture? When mosquitoes seem less active? When bats first comb the night sky? Better be more diligent if I want any answers. Better watch and record. Write it all down. Each and every moment. Here, try it:

…Dusk falls by the minute, hiding the grain of the deck's planks. My empty dinner plate glows. A rustle in the brush downhill. Something also breaking the pond's surface, concentric circles spreading, fading… To the north, night clouds ignite, heat lightning the color of creamsicles. To the east, the moon finally rises, yellow and a few days shy of full… Through my binoculars loom its great lunar craters and ancient seas. Men have walked there, have actually walked there… No doubt it's shining down on Manhattan, too. That old and steady glow. That pull…

Civics

About two weeks into my residence, I came out onto the schoolhouse deck one morning and found a plain envelope, held down by a rock. In it was a folded note from my new landlord Tina Bourjaily, who lived downhill in the white house with the willows across the road. She wrote, "...here is a key to your house, if you would like to lock it; for the south door. The other one fits the padlock on the gate for times it may be locked." At the bottom of the envelope lay two keys—one shiny, one tarnished.

Funny, I hadn't even thought to ask for keys.

The presence of the letter meant Tina was up and out for her daily woodswalks earlier than me. She was stoic in her regimen, near devout. I'd noticed her hiking toward dusk as well, her silvered hair, her strident step, her two small dogs trailing behind. She could slip into the landscape as surely as this letter had into its envelope. The only other form of correspondence we'd shared was a hand-typed lease, similarly offered as an afterthought. Its scant paragraph simply mentioned rent, utilities, and duration. No forms in triplicate, no credit checks, no security deposits—none of the typical graft and gridlock of New York City landlords. Actually, there seemed a degree of embarrassment on both Tina and my parts in affixing our signatures. Whatever her criteria were for judging a potential tenant I can't say, but as for me, this was the first time in my life paying rent was an absolute joy.

I continued reading her brief note and between its few lines glimpsed many messages. Of how Tina was considering my reactions as a newcomer to country living, of certain pragmatic needs that living entailed, and a conferring of some of those responsibilities. The quiet placement of the envelope at the far corner of the porch also hinted at her not wanting to intrude on my privacy. Though our homes were within eyeshot, solid stands of trees and brush stood between us, which suited me fine. Tina too, I sensed. After all, she was also choosing to live out here alone. She must have had her reasons as well.

At the close of her note, came a short postscript—"It makes me happy you are in residence here"—plain speak for a Plains landscape. To my Easterner's ear she may have seemed to mince words, but certainly not meanings. Despite our solitudes, Tina was already sharing a great deal with me, risking part of her homestead—a trust I wanted to be careful not to breach by any oversights. Or undue distances.

That afternoon, I went into the woods and picked a bowlful of blackberries for her in appreciation. I telephoned first then headed downhill, where I found Tina seated in her house's large mudroom, squarely atop a wooden chair from which she did not rise when I entered. She did not speak at first either, motioning for me to take the only other chair in the room. On her lap was a small dog, from whose thick black hair she was painstakingly combing out burrs. Another similar brown one lay panting at her feet. I studied their little faces and pushed-in noses.

"King Charles'," Tina finally said, "a breed once favored by the English Court. Show dogs."

She pulled several clumps of dark fur from her comb's metal tines and added to a growing mound on the short table between us. I set down my small bowl of choice blackberries. Tina nodded at them, as if they were an acceptable tithe.

"Do you show them?" I asked.

"These two? Oh no, they're too jittery. I rescued them from an Alabama litter of seven. Abused as pups, as you can see."

The brown one had been cowering and steadily growling under its breath since I arrived.

"Now you stop that," scolded Tina. "Enough."

She exchanged dogs on her lap and the snarling became a chorus, both vying for Tina's attention. I was relieved to see it wasn't my presence alone that set them on edge. I already knew what at least one thought of me—that morning its own spare missive was deposited on the schoolhouse deck not far from Tina's letter.

"That's better now. Good dog."

Tina worked the comb against the matted hair of the brown dog's belly, and it practically started purring. I wondered if she'd gone all the way to Alabama to buy these dogs. My family always got our mutts from the local pound. I looked about the mudroom, which in Tina's house was huge compared to the schoolhouse's tiny vestibule. Its floor was raw wood, the walls lined with boot racks, riding crops and brittle halters, an old croquet set. In the corner hung a metal bucket filled with rusted scrap, strung as a counterweight to her basement's trapdoor. On the window ledge perched a pile of tomatoes, still fresh with garden dust. Tina tore at the metal tines of the comb, a new brown pile of hair taking form on the table.

"So, you've lived here all your life?" I asked.

"No, just thirty odd years. I used to live in New York, London, Spain ..."

I'd heard Tina's ex-husband was Vance Bourjaily, who once taught at the Iowa Writers' Workshop. His reputation held a certain hush and pedigree from the early 1960s, having been critically named alongside Norman Mailer as one of

Hemingway's heirs apparent. I also heard the schoolhouse had once served as his writing studio.

"But I'm from Nebraska originally," said Tina.

"Really?"

"My grandfather used to run a mill there. Supplied settlers with pack mules and lumber. Back when Nebraska was the edge of the frontier."

Tina shifted the dog on her lap.

"Yes. Interesting man. At the age of seventy-nine he started feeling crowded and pushed out west once again. Packed up his family and all his holdings onto the Union Pacific and headed for Idaho ... Seventy-nine, imagine."

Her voice was tinged with both awe and a faint resignation. I gauged Tina as somewhere in her mid-sixties. Still, the word "frontier" seemed to echo in the room. I tried to picture an elderly man standing beside the rails, a little stoop-shouldered yet proud, his life gradually filling a train. The gush of white steam hissing out onto the platform, momentarily engulfing a passing boy's knickers. Outside Tina's window, a breeze sifted through the backyard's marsh grass, rolling back toward trees lining Old Man's Creek. *Uncrowded*, I thought, and my gaze slowly returned to her face.

Perhaps it was the steel and silver of her hair, or her skin so thick and lined, or those ardent eyes, set deep and blue as any prairie sky. Or perhaps it was the light—the way it streaked through her mudroom's wall of windows at that particular time of day—fixing each of her features into portrait, her twin canines flanking. In any event, for an instant I caught a glimpse of something if not necessarily royal, then certainly stately. A first inkling that this landscape of mud and marsh grass into which I'd stumbled was in its own way groomed and stewarded by a breed of quiet, solid nobility. That it might stand at the edge of some frontier for me.

16 August. The air started smelling familiar this morning… Working on my maps and writing today. Already feeling a bit proprietary. Imagine that. Plucked off some vines climbing up the deck's rail. Called jewelweed. Such a conflicted name. Its speckled flowers have a strange and hooded design, with what looks like a downturned tail at their end. Who's to say what is and isn't a weed? What is and isn't native, marginal? Stuck a few clipped blossoms in a mug on the windowsill near my bed. Bringing some color inside.

At the public library I found one local map color-coded according to how sunlight reflected off Johnson County's respective ground cover. The palette wasn't very wide—a patchwork quilt of corn, pasture, and soybean. Otherwise, there were loose blue threads for rivers and creeks, and at center what looked like a bleach stain representing Iowa City—spreading yet well-contained. From one year's map to the next certain green and yellow squares shifted with crop rotation, but the overall pattern held steady. Nowhere on these maps, however, was there any indication of the schoolhouse.

Nor could I find any reference to elevation on these maps. With over ninety percent of Iowa's land given to agriculture, one's focus here was almost entirely horizontal. Whatever few buildings there were poked up like untended outcroppings among the flat fields, and the state's highest point, 1670 feet, wasn't even celebrated.

In a way, all of Iowa could be seen as one huge floodplain between two of the nation's greatest rivers. A motorist passing through on Interstate 80 barely needed to detour for any cities—Davenport sprouted to the east along the banks of the Mississippi, Des Moines about midway across, and to the west Council Bluffs just before crossing the mighty Missouri. On north-south interstates there were even less obstructions. And frankly, passing through Iowa was what many motorists did, often without stopping for gas. I'd overheard an elderly woman at a truck stop say, "You know the best thing about Iowa, don't you? Well, wherever you're going, you're about halfway there."

Yet I wasn't going anywhere. For once, it felt like my map, my running, could stop.

Back home from the library, I re-considered how truly rare the schoolhouse's four hundred ninety-six acres of unfarmed land were in this section of Johnson County. How truly lucky I was to be living there and helping look after them. How documenting my days might offer my budding fiction writing practice another dimension.

As for my journal's charting of Redbird Farm, the more land I walked, the more I felt obliged to record. All its hills and trails and paths and ponds kept pulling me deeper and deeper in. One day, a maze of briars parted to reveal a slight bluff whose ridges fanned out like knuckles and fingers crawling down toward a barren floodplain—beyond which lay the property line of Old Man's Creek's northern branch. I struggled to sketch in all these subtle elevations and transitions, but my sheet of paper quickly grew overrun with straggly lines. I tried adding colors to help, but quit when it started looking too much like a New York City subway map.

Instead, I began numbering successive pages like in a road atlas, creating a grid I intended to eventually tape up onto the schoolhouse wall. I'd buy pushpins and make little red flags, claim each territory piece by piece. Each day I'd duly set out to map one section of the property, but invariably get sidetracked. The texture of a leaf bottom, the coo of a bird, the scent of musk—everything and anything bore investigation. Page after journal page unfurled, their catalogue of minute descriptions and observations soon outdistancing my map lines.

I remember a hitchhiker once told me there was no adventure in maps. To which I would like to add, no greater understanding either. No doubt I could plod on with this ever more minute mapping of Redbird Farm. I could draft each and every curve of crag and creek and timber, I could circle the globe chasing my myopic dreams of Magellan, yet would it bring me any closer to knowing where I belonged?

I flipped through the field guides I'd borrowed from the library, matching their photographs to my last few days' notes and sightings. That helix of seedpod belonged to the Honey Locust, that flash of yellow wing in midair, called Flicker.

"Bloodroot," I called out.

"Kestrel."

"Trefoil."

"Nuthatch."

I recited each one aloud to the schoolhouse walls, garnering each name like some Cub Scout earning badges. Albeit a Cub Scout with a receding hairline.

Yet there they were to discover, on the page and on the ridge: the backward thorns of Multiflora Rose; the gentle bow of flowering Yarrow in a ditch; the darting yellow wingbeats of a Goldfinch. Each and every thing had a precise name, and a specific place among the larger quilt. A specific role to play. And in a way, there I was too, recording them all first-hand. Sometimes I'd stop in midfield, in mid stride, and pinch myself.

While growing up in New York, this time of year had always brought a sad, sinking feeling to my stomach. Summer vacation days waning and the dreaded return of September suddenly tangible. Back To School signs coloring storefronts. Back to school—how I'd always hated that.

But this schoolhouse was different. This was *finally* different.

First of September. 7 AM. Need a sweatshirt today. Foxtail grass is in seed, their white haloes bobbing with the breeze. And the Queen Anne's lace's umbrella blooms, listing between tiny spider webs, morning's dew strung like pearls. Amazing how each day these spiders can wholly re-create their homes...Meanwhile, the edges of ivy on the schoolhouse are starting to blush. Downhill, treetops flicker with the underside of leaves. The sky darkening. Between crow calls, thunder rolls from south to west. This must be where weather begins.

One Sunday morning, Tina asked if I'd help replace gaps of rotted planks in the fencing that wound down the schoolhouse hill to the front gate. Evidently hunting season was approaching and untended fence lines were an invitation to trespass. I carried the boards from her barn across the road and sawed them to length. The local oak was hard and needed pre-drilling for nail holes. It felt good to sweat and work with my hands, to measure things out precisely.

At first Tina stood nearby, checking over my shoulder, then gradually receded to eye each plank from a distance before I nailed it to the post.

"How's this, Tina?"

Again and again she'd dip her chin and squint from under the shadow of her straw hat.

"A touch lower," she'd say.

"Now?"

"Now."

I drove the nail and headed back to the sawhorses. Tina drew a wrist across her forehead then turned downhill.

"Just remember," she said over her shoulder, "a hand level's fine, but the lay of the land has the last word."

I recognized her leaving me to work alone as another token of trust. As she followed the line of mended fence downhill, I wondered whether my helping keep others out meant I now belonged within? Wondered what it was that had made Tina and Vance choose this particular spot as their home ground? And if he'd left, why she'd remained?

Overhead, the early autumn sky hung as silent as it was blue. I tacked another plank to post and stepped back to gauge its level with the land, the weight of the hammer balanced in my palm. A sudden wave swept through me, a sense of what it must feel like to own and be owned by a single plot of land. Of why people sometimes fought and even died for their allotted tract. Why sons and, yes, lovers didn't abandon its hearth.

I wondered, too, about my apartment back in New York, about Sybil. Over the years there was surely more to our relationship than just sex and cinema. While I'd never set foot in her home, I had met her sons and watched them grow from a distance. She even got pregnant once, though we wisely aborted. So I had shared in some of her other life; her hopes, her concerns, her fears. Once, she even joked about me pushing her around in a wheelchair someday—a joke that elicited nervous laughter from both of us. So while moment-to-moment we remained committed to one another, our denial of the future left notions of duties and obligations up in the air. As always, freedom bears a weight.

In Iowa, a mere town or two away bearded Amish were hitching their horses to wagons, one hundred and fifty years of history still visible and moving across the land's face. I'd parked my car along their dirt roads and watched them harvesting and bundling hay by hand. Sat outside their fence lines and wondered what such commitment might shape and sprout within me. For all my miles of traveling, with or without Sybil, I had to admit any true glimpse of an inner landscape still eluded me. Any true test of a deeper connection. An intimacy that could grow. A real rootedness.

Do we inhabit borders, or do they inhabit us?

Before coming to Iowa, I'd happened on an article in the Sunday *New York Times* concerning the Midwest. How the term itself was nebulous. Though there seemed little doubt Iowa was at its center, no one could quite agree on its exact perimeter. Did it include Ohio and Michigan? Exclude the Dakotas? Ultimately, the article could only conclude the Midwest wasn't so much a geography of states as it was a state of mind. A state of heart.

The heartland. This too was a term I'd heard the Midwest called, and in all truth why I'd probably pointed the car toward Iowa in the first place. For deep down I knew, above all else, I'd landed here because something in my heart had lost its footing. Something that didn't point to bearings so much as to what I couldn't bear.

Spelling

When I was growing up, my mother always used to take photographs of me on the first day of school. With a new shirt tucked into my pants and hair combed to one side, I'd stand out in front of our house and wait for her to compose the image. At that time of year the mimosa tree overhead was always in bloom, its pink puffs dangling. "Look down, look down honey," she'd say, which was always hard because of the morning sun. Some years she'd realize there was no film in the camera and would have to run back inside the house.

While waiting, I'd practice poses, trying to look like my television heroes—those brave and dashing cowboys on *Bonanza* and *The Rifleman*—like someone I wasn't. When my mother returned, she'd wrestle with loading the film then I'd finally hear the click of the Kodak and could stop worrying about who I was.

We never actually laid out those pictures side by side. Instead, from year to year we'd joke about which was growing faster, the mimosa or me. My mother, however, was not as shortsighted as she then appeared to me. In retrospect, I realized her intent was quite meditated—not only to record the early chapters of a small and squinting boy, but to preserve them. Somewhere in her basement, deep in some dresser draw or shoebox, that document still exists.

My family, you see, had a tendency to hold on to things. My father, a Depression-era child, couldn't abide any waste. An electrical engineer, he could and would fix anything rather than see it thrown away. I remember our basement shelves lined with old mayonnaise jars and coffee cans chock full of screws and nuts, washers, wheels, springs, any spare hardware you could possibly name. Dad's workbench was always strewn with a skeletal TV chassis and voltmeter, vacuum tubes and resistors. Oftentimes we'd be driving in his car and he'd pull right over to the curbside trash, brandishing screwdrivers and pliers to scavenge anything salvageable. After all, you never knew when you might need something.

My mother, meanwhile, was a secretary, and hence very good at filing things away. She held tight to her own brand of treasures—photographs and memories and magazines and even her maternity clothes—but for other reasons.

So it came as no surprise I felt a similar urge to preserve what I was experiencing at the schoolhouse. The words in my journal could only capture so much, so one early morning I stepped out onto the deck with my camera in-hand. I started composing a shot but as with my maps found it impossible to encompass my entire backyard within a single frame. Instead, I began snapping successive pictures, starting due west and slowly pivoting toward sunrise until I'd caught a sufficient panorama of my precious pond and pasture and hillside.

I then photographed the schoolhouse itself. Placed at the right edge of the frame with the cast of rising sun dappling its ivy-covered face, the very building seemed to blossom from the surrounding green. A breeze sifted through the line of pine trees over my head, their needles quivering like those delicate mimosa blossoms of my youth. If I closed my eyes I could still see their precise pink hue, their flutter. Every year they came like a promise. Every September, another chance to start anew.

Back indoors, I steeped a cup of tea and sat on the couch to clean my camera lens. Across from me spread the schoolhouse's stone fireplace, its thin mantle graced by two brass ornaments shaped like horses with curling fish tails. I'd spotted them when I first arrived at the schoolhouse, and literally shivered. Typically, such figures only flanked the passenger seat on

Venetian gondolas, yet here they stood a thousand miles from any sea. The sheen of their brass played off the charred hearth and I reached for my camera again.

While composing a close-up, I noticed something embedded in the resin-coated stone below the mantle. A shape, no a letter. It looked like a "D", and nearby hid another. I got a knife from the kitchen and started scraping away at the obscured message. D - O - L, it spelled. DOLCE F - A ... *Dolce Far Niente*— Italian!

I fell back onto the couch, trying to puzzle it out. If Tina had once been to Italy to buy the brass horses, no doubt she could have come across such an idiom. *Dolce Far Niente* (Doing Nothing Is Sweet) was a phrase I too had picked up in Venice, where it practically became my credo. And wouldn't it make the perfect motto for idle winter nights here, lounging before a burning fire? I stared at the fireplace's inscription for a long time, mouthing each individual letter again as if I were in some Spelling Bee, as if trying to decipher some deeper code.

At the university, I was similarly trying to unravel what made certain writers more affecting than others. By now my second year in the MFA program was underway, yet there still seemed so much to learn. Long gone were any lofty ideas of inspiration and innate talent in deference to a more grounded and tangible process. We talked of hands-on tools and techniques, of breaking down our works-in-progress in terms of their whole and component parts. Our writing desks became workbenches, places where we had to keep redesigning and redrafting until we could construct a sound and solid tale. We were toiling at a trade. No wonder they called it a "workshop."

In short, what made good writers was good writing, period. And what made good writing was practice. Attending to the way your words worked on the page. Period.

Back home at the schoolhouse, I'd sit out on its deck stirring my morning tea and mulling over this idea of a story's building blocks. Across the way, several horses were strolling down from the high pasture, their staggered shapes forming a loose column, not unlike words falling into place in a sentence. I noted another two-legged figure trailing them in the landscape, like a period. Probably Andre, who boarded these horses at Redbird. Tina had introduced us the week prior, if only briefly. I left my empty cup on the deck rail and walked downhill to the barn. Before I could even say hello, Andre had a grooming brush in my hand.

"Well," he said, "horse is waiting."

I took three steps forward and stood breathless. Despite all my childhood's fantasizing about TV cowboys, I'd never actually been this close to a horse. I stared at the raised veins straining against its skin, a sudden twitch in its shoulder. Finally I reached out and touched the brush to the horse's back. Dust rose from its chestnut coat, the smell of animal filling the air.

Andre stepped up cradling a saddle on one forearm.

"So. You ride?" he asked in his thick Serbian accent.

"No," I said.

"Never?"

I shook my head. "Just bicycles."

He waved his hand before him as if swatting at a fly then handed me a dusty blanket. I thought for a moment then swung it over the horse's back.

"No, higher," said Andre. He saddled the mare and eased the bit between her teeth, swiftly curling the bridle over her ears. "Now come, I show you."

I followed him out the barn to the small arena figuring I'd watch him ride, but Andre didn't mount. He led the horse in a small circle and stopped near a wooden box at the corral's center.

"Well," he said again.

"Me?"

"How else you learn?"

I stood very still, watching the horse jostle her head against the reins.

"What, you afraid?" asked Andre.

"No," I said, but didn't step forward. More out of respect than fear, I told myself.

"So then, come. Horse is waiting."

I stepped up onto the box, my knees unsteady.

"Left leg," said Andre.

"Now," said Andre.

It was as if I were a marionette. I have no memory of making a choice, of moving my own body, yet there I was, suddenly straddling those high flanks. Andre hooked the stirrups up out of the way and stepped back.

"So. Legs down, toes up slightly but relaxed. Arms out, swing. Swing your arms! Good. Now eyes, follow them. Arms up, eyes to the sky, now lean out over mane and down. Good, good, now swing your legs."

Andre's directions came at me like clipped military orders, hinting at what Tina told me about his having fought for both the Yugoslavs and the French Resistance. I was trying to do everything he said, trying not to think about how high off the ground I was.

"Good. Now, look. The horse's front legs do nothing but place. The motor system is here, in back," and he touched a crop to the mare's haunch and suddenly she was moving. I grabbed for her mane.

"No. Arms at sides," ordered Andre.

He led us in a circle, no reins no stirrups, helping me gain my basic balance first. We did two laps.

"Good, now close your eyes."

I did as I was told. Behind me I heard the flick of the crop and a dark world jolted beneath me. I pressed in with my knees.

"Good, good. Okay, open your eyes and put stirrups down. Now practice going up and down. Up and down. No, no, not like that. Don't bounce, touch. It's like with woman, you slide up and ease down. You married?"

"No," I said.

"Divorced?"

"No."

"What's wrong with you?"

I couldn't answer that, even if I wasn't concentrating so hard on a horse.

"Well, there is someone," I began, "but she, we …"

How could I possibly explain my relationship with Sybil to him, to anyone really? That she was the one who was married— or rather estranged from her husband, if not technically divorced. How could I ever spell it all out so it made any sense in the real world? Even my best friends couldn't figure out what kept us together. Our equation was simply a given, at least where we were concerned. Where we were concerned, we were living a fiction.

" … It's a long story," I finally said.

"Yes. All stories like this are long. But now we try posting, no?"

The whip snapped and the horse started trotting. I struggled against the movement, fighting it, Andre barking out his orders. For the most part I was merely holding on, but once or twice I released to the horse's rhythm and felt a sudden yet smooth burst forward. Frightening, yet freeing too.

After three or so laps Andre led the horse back to the ring's center, and with much reluctance I slid back down to earth. In my head, though, I was tall as a cowpoke in the saddle. Andre nodded, then quickly mounted and galloped off in a cloud of dust—just like on TV, his broad back silhouetted against the horizon. Maybe in Iowa I could be a cowboy after all, I thought. A frontiersman.

12 September. Afternoon. Taking a break from mowing the hillside on Tina's little 110 John Deere. Next to its throttle, instead of settings for SLOW and FAST are pictures of a turtle and a hare. The smell of cut clover, sweet. Bird's-foot trefoil, crown vetch—learning all these groundcovers' names. Crickets by the thousands jump in the clippings. Clouds gathering to the north. Better hit it boy, the "back forty" are waiting …

Evening. Dirt tired. Took a swim after mowing, maybe the last of the season. Pond water getting cold, even at the surface. Found out from Tina that each pond has a name: Schoolhouse, Woods, Upper and Lower, and on the far side of the pasture two more—60 Acres and Number Ten. The last named after a cow that once drowned in it. Anyway, went fishing at Woods Pond and pulled in a bluegill the first time my lure touched water! And now, two bass fillets steaming on the barbecue in a pan with green onions and ginger. Deck table all set, like for some romantic date … a citronella candle, a little white wine, a little sunset … Oh yes, and would you care for a little pepper on that, sir?

"Fiction does its work by creating a dream in the reader's mind," wrote John Gardner, further explaining how the dream needed to remain "continuous" throughout the course of your storytelling. The more fully you could inhabit the world and skin of your characters, the more honestly you might render their fictive realities on the page. This made perfect sense to me, not unlike how I'd heard theater actors prepared for their roles on stage.

Many an evening I'd pace around the schoolhouse couch reciting my drafts aloud, trying to embody each character's voice and mannerisms, but also noting the movement and rhythm of the words themselves. And I found following the flow of my sentences felt a bit like circling that corral down by the barn on horseback—sometimes awkward and bumpy, sometimes smooth and natural.

Apart from an ugly old couch, the only other furniture in the schoolhouse when I moved in was its huge limestone slab dining table at center and a wooden rocking chair. Instinctively, I wanted to keep things sparse and simple. To create an open and unencumbered space just for thinking. Just me, and words.

Each day, though, something from my woodswalks found its way back to the schoolhouse for further study. A lichen-covered branch. A blue feather. A gnawed black walnut. An abandoned wasps' nest. I set up two sawhorses and a few extra fence planks in one corner of the room as a research station. Special finds started to grace each window ledge and wall, a sort of rotating exhibit. I told myself I wasn't building a collection, but rather a vocabulary.

One night, however, I happened to be out on the deck stargazing when I paused outside the schoolhouse's side door. Inside glowed a yellow lamp casting shadows among all my books and papers, my gathered bouquets of drying milkweed and thistle hanging on the walls, the scavenged bird nests and seed corn and old brown medicine bottles lining the windowsills. I stood there and peered in as if at the life of some hoarding pack rat or bowerbird. Some stranger. Some costume shop.

I recall my grandfather once saying: "A man must wear many hats in his life." This wasn't even my hat-maker grandfather, whom I'd never met, but my maternal grandfather, the kosher butcher. For most of his life he wore that butcher's hat, though I'd heard he'd always longed to work with fabrics. Evidently he loved clothes, and in the evenings would don silk shirts and plush pants with pleats ironed to such perfection his children weren't allowed to sit on his lap. In the evenings, my grandfather would simply shed his stained apron and become another man.

Of course one could say he wore other hats, too. Those of a Pole, a Jew, an immigrant, a proud American. A democrat and a gambler. A son, brother, husband, father, and, finally, the embittered widower who moved in with us before he died. In my brief time with him, however, he wasn't any of those things, but rather the man who taught me how to play gin rummy. A man who ate pike fish on a yellow plate and drank tea from a glass. Who stared at his little black and white television set each night, and sucked oxygen from a green tank in the corner of his room.

Memory is selective. More so than one's fate often is, it would seem. As limited as the labels we come to assign ourselves—little letters we inscribe on our business cards, and tombstones. Our sentences. A man ought to be free to handle cloth instead of meat. Free to choose or exchange hats. Yet in so doing, does he *really* change? Would I, out here in Iowa?

Heading downhill to check for mail one afternoon, I noticed Andre's blue station wagon parked beside the gate, as usual. Closer to the barn, however, sat a strange pickup with a rusted horseshoe welded to its hood. I walked over.

"Ah, our newest horseman," Andre said to me. "Meet Dick Harris."

A greying man glanced up from within the barn's shadows, a dozen square nail heads poking out from the corner of his mouth, an upturned hoof leaning against his lower thigh. The horse behind him shifted weight.

"Easy buddy, easy," he said. "Just set on me. Stay right on me."

Damn, I thought, a blacksmith. A real blacksmith. Dick pulled gently on the gelding's tail and with the other hand held the horseshoe in place with his pinkie and pointer. He tapped in a nail halfway, then a second. "Hush now, bad time to mess up, hush boy." He gave another little tug at the horse's tail, now in his mouth, swiftly hammered in the front nails, then followed suit all around the hoof.

"All right take a little break now, boy."

After ambling over, he said, "So, you're a horseman, are you?"

He was a good half-foot shorter than me, but his handshake made me wince.

"No," I said, "Andre gave me my first lesson a couple weeks ago. I'm just learning."

Dick nodded once, then kept walking over toward his anvil.

"Mind if I watch?" I asked.

"Hell no. Suit yourself."

He wheeled over a little cart, and I questioned him on the names of his tools: the clinch block and snippers, protractor, calipers. Back alongside the gelding, he slid the block into place against the horse's hoof, bent each clinch over and snipped off their points. To smooth them down, he held the file between a thumb and forefinger, pivoting only from the elbow. Meanwhile, Andre led over the matching mare of the team.

"Are you my good friend," he cooed into her ear, then handed over her reins.

"Now this mare here," said Dick, "looks a little short in the pastern. She's showing a lot of toe, too. Probably that dry June and wet July."

He quickly clipped the old bent clinches and pried off one of her shoes, then cut a width of hoof nail with a slow sweep of his wrist and knife.

"That's why she hasn't been breaking over for you, Andre. See?"

Andre nodded and I followed suit, though had no idea what they were talking about. Dick shaved off another crescent of toe, then reached for a different file from the cart. His hands moved as precisely as a surgeon's: caliper, protractor, file, protractor. He was setting this mare's hooves at 54°, explaining how the figures were based on angles with the floor and the horse's pastern and shoulder. I pulled out a piece of mail from my back pocket and started writing down everything he said on the back of an envelope.

He looked at me oddly then glanced toward Andre.

"He's a student, you know. Writing student."

"Riding? At the university?" asked Dick.

"Uh, no. Write-ing," I admitted.

Dick bent from the waist over the scattered horseshoes on the floor, his hands holding on to his knees.

"Yeah well, guess they got schools for everything now. Even shoeing. First one was right here in Iowa, you know. Nowadays you got Jim Keith's down in Tucumcarie. Roy Evans in Macomb ... Me, I learned from my father."

He gathered up the shoes and straightened with effort, as if lifting his whole legacy. The belt buckle at his waist hung oval and worn almost beyond reading: 1959 BULL RIDING, LEWISTOWN MONTANA. I watched him hold up one shoe perpendicular to the sky then squint. Here was someone practicing a real trade with cast iron tools, not some "fiction writer" with a flimsy pencil point. Dick bounced his sledge off the anvil and let its own weight drop on the curved metal. The ring of authenticity, crisp and echoing.

29 September. First frost. The hillside's a carpet of glitter. Steam rising a full fifteen feet above Schoolhouse Pond, rusting the cattails. The ash leaves turned sallow overnight, the poison sumac red. Blackberry

brambles reduced to naked clusters of stump and thorn. My fingers
cramping now, too. Shivering between seasons...

Got two letters today—one from Sybil, which I've yet to open, and
one from San Francisco, from Alessandro. He sounds okay, getting
back on his feet again. Said he found another apartment not far from
Lua's, and a couple of part-time cooking jobs. Hasn't seen or spoken to
her in weeks, their divorce all but paperwork now... So strange, the
way both of us are now apart from the women we love, and both in
foreign lands... He wrote, "learning to live alone has been good for
me," but between the lines I can tell he's still depressed. His T-cell count
is holding steady though, which is probably the most important news.
Hard to imagine him living with HIV day to day. That kind of REAL
weight hanging overhead. Surreal. Now there's one you can't simply
run away from... It seems so unfair. All from just partying, his simple
sharing of a needle...

Near midnite. Horses right outside the windows. Andre moved them
to my side of the hill today for fresh pasture. Can hear them rubbing
up against the deck, scratching forelocks. Now and then the dull tamp
of their hooves, sudden snorts. New rhythms in the dark... Time for
dreams now... galloping gondole... cowboys... centaurs

When I'd first arrived in Italy, I wasn't entirely alone. My friend
Lua was already living there, and put me in touch with the
language institute in Venice. Over the years she'd become my
inadvertent employment agent, as I'd followed her into jobs
at a Montessori school and the air charter discounter in New
York, then across the ocean. At that juncture, Lua was happily
engaged to Alessandro and working in a small children's theater

company based in Verona, where she acted and Aless ran lights. I took a shine to him immediately, and not only for his easy humor or the sly glint in his eye. Some other kind of fraternity flowed between us—almost as if he could've been an older brother.

Born and raised in Venice, Aless knew the labyrinth of its canals well, and one day when he and Lua were visiting his family, he offered to take me out rowing. He taught me my first oar strokes, taught me where and when to shift my weight, and when and where to stop for the freshest local vino. Yet above all, what I imbibed that day was a first inkling that inside a maze I needn't feel lost so much as liquid—flowing forth, seeking my own level, trusting that all my floating about might have some direction after all.

Coming to Iowa to study fiction writing was probably the first vocational choice I'd made of my own accord. One afternoon while at the university, a classmate stopped me in the hallway.

"What the hell is that?" he said pointing at my chest.

"My new vest."

I'd found it recently at a local yard sale. I bought almost all my clothes used, partly because of finances but partly due to my general feelings about consumption. I was my father's son, after all. Waste not, want not.

"No, that," said my classmate, and jabbed a finger at the patch on my vest's breast pocket.

I tilted my head and read the letters upside down: C-O-O-P encircled in red and blue, above the words, "CROP PRODUCTION."

"For Christ sakes, you're from Brooklyn, Marc. BROOK-LYN."

He walked away, nearly cackling. I looked down at the vest's polyester hugging my waist, my worn jeans caked with mud at the ankles, my boots leaving small clumps behind me. Down the hallway my classmate's laughter echoed off the walls. Who'd I think I was, Daniel Boone? The country wasn't something you could don at will. Farming was in the blood, and land inherited. Or at least earned over time. Humility, too.

So perhaps all this woodswalking and role-playing *was* mere appropriation on my part. Or worse still, an arrogant masquerade. I recalled similar thoughts arising after my having lived several months in Italy. Fluent enough by then to share in some of the local dialect, I fancied myself a Venetian. One day I was traveling to Verona to visit Lua and Alessandro when I saw an image in the passing landscape, framed by the train's window. No town, no road. Just a man, a horse, and the horizon. Having no other clue, I imagined him a horse thief.

Out in the open Iowa countryside, I wondered if I'd now become that man myself. A man leading a horse? A thief? A mirage? A *fiction*? After all, I'd learned the term was also used in coin collecting—a fictive coin was a counterfeit.

That night, I got back from classes and lay on the schoolhouse couch staring above the fireplace at those scraped

Italian letters, set in stone. Nearby hung the panoramas I'd been documenting, each wide strip of photos tacked one below the other. Scanning down the wall, I could discern a story beginning to unfold—one in which the trees were slowly changing their colors and starting to undress. I thought of that old mimosa tree again, and how among my mother's memorabilia its fragile blossoms must still be dangling over my head. I knew other photographs of me as a boy also lay in those dusty shoeboxes, many in which I wore hats—firemen's hats and ski hats, cowboy hats—a fantasy phase I thought I'd outgrown.

Maybe not.

Then, of course, I thought of Sybil. Was it possible I'd made up our relationship as well? Our whole time together an illusion, a fake?

On a near bookshelf was wedged an envelope, thick with photographs. I got up from the couch and pulled them out, flipping through the whole stack of images, one by one: Sybil in Central Park and out at Coney Island. In Italy and Corfu and Oslo. The Outer Banks. I could recall each and every one's precise framing—as if I were once again squinting through the camera's viewfinder, struggling to capture the gentle curve in her cheeks. Or the sway of her crazed black locks in the breeze. Or her length of neckline, tapering into her lapels. Her bottomless eyes. Again and again, I'd struggled to fix her elusive essence on film. To somehow hold on to it forever.

Desperately I thumbed through the stack until I reached one in which she and I stood pictured together—taken at Lua and Alessandro's wedding. I confirmed her fingers wrapped round my waist, mine enfolding her wrist. I could conjure each feature, each hug and tiny gesture between us, and I swear not a one of them ever felt posed. No, our love was no mirage. No fantasy, no fiction. Certainly that was self-evident in these photos. There was much we were denying, but not that.

I glanced at the telephone, halfway across the room. It would be so easy to dial her number, to go back to her, back to our beautiful bubble.

I stared on at my stack of photos. There lay the proof, all spread before me and plainly spelled out in Kodacolor, in Black & White. I wasn't only holding on to her. I was terrified of letting go.

Reading

Sometimes while staring at a page in a book I'll suddenly stop in mid-sentence, stumbling over a word I've known and used for years. At that moment though, it will appear like a strange stone in the path and I'm not really sure what it means. So before proceeding, I need to go back and redefine terms.

At the schoolhouse this was almost a daily occurrence, the dictionary quickly becoming the most visited book on my shelf. Again and again I'd flip through its worn pages, searching for sense and clarity, yet all the while feeling like something was still beyond my grasp. I started to sense the true meaning of language might not necessarily reside within any given definition so much as in the words themselves, in the way they could pass through air between people.

Webster's definition for *communicate* stated, "to convey knowledge or information, to reveal by clear signs, symbols, or behavior." It derived from the Latin *communicatus* or *communicare*, meaning to impart or participate. A little further down the dictionary column came the word *communion*, also from the Latin *communio*, or mutual participation. An act or instance of sharing.

In other words, a kind of intimacy. A faith.

For the first few months I lived in Venice, I recall walking around with a dictionary in my hip pocket. The only Italian I'd known before my arrival were menu basics—*pesto* and *parmigiana*, *saltimbocca*. Indeed the language of food proved some of the first vocabulary I needed to learn. Hunger, it seems, is always a quick study. I remember wandering around the Rialto market furtively staring at all the fruit and vegetable stalls, trying to translate metrics, always buying too much. The merchants loved me, saw me coming a kilometer away. So I wandered more and more, studying street signs and store windows, and gradually the maze of city and syntax was deciphered and imbibed.

One day, I stepped into Venice's Jewish Ghetto and felt a faint familiarity. The oldest in the world, it's where the term "ghetto" first derived. I'd gone there merely as a cultural tourist, yet within its dank synagogue walls heard certain chants and melodies I remembered from childhood. The lilt and pull of those echoes caught me off guard, for the synagogue as a place of worship had never worked for me. Judaism's codes of ethics and social responsibility struck me as credible, but not its wrathful God. The people who stood beside me in Venice's Old Ghetto were of no blood or spiritual relation whatsoever, yet somehow we were woven into the same story of a migrant culture over five thousand years in the making—that of the "Wandering Jew." Well, at least I could connect with the wandering part.

At the same time I frequented the city's many churches. Initially drawn to their art and architecture, I began to linger among their humble pews and reliquaries. Overhead, incense thinned into vaulting archways and cupolas, where glittering mosaics rendered gospels for the once illiterate masses. And ever so slowly, I too sensed an awareness seeping into my own limited comprehension.

I first felt it at the Frari, one of Venice's major Franciscan cathedrals. At the time I was bathing in the glow of Titian's "Assumption," which rose in all its glory behind the main altar. On one side of me sat a hunchback monk and on the other a German art student sketching in her pad—the three of us pure strangers, yet collectively transfixed, reverent. Weeks later, I sensed it again under the dim shadows of Veronese's brushwork, seated among a penitent chorus of old widows and kneeling stevedores at the church of San Nicolo dei Mendicoli. Or then there was one Sunday morning I took a boat across the *bacino* to the Benedictine San Giorgio Maggiore in search of a Carpaccio painting, yet at the top of a circular stairwell found a small, hidden chapel instead. Inside, a tiny mass was underway and I can still recall the deep purple of the priest's vestments, the soft face of an elderly Japanese woman perched nearby on a pew, the faint echo of footsteps out in the courtyard.

It was another church, however, perched alongside a canal not far from the train station that became my favorite sanctuary. Or not a church, but a temple housing the remains of Santa Lucia, virgin and martyr, patron saint of the blind. In the furthest apse lay her mummified corpse, stolen from her native Sicily centuries ago and never returned. For a groping myopic like me, she became my adopted *patrona*.

Almost weekly I'd come and lean my forehead against the large glass case that preserved her shrouded relics—a white gown pristinely draped over her torso, a silvered mask suggesting her sleeping visage. I'd close my own eyes too, and just stand there, the hum of boat engines sifting through the stone walls, the circle of my breath condensing on the glass. I had no idea what I was doing, what precisely I was waiting for, but I came often. For me the ritual had nothing whatsoever to do with any religious dogma or even prayer. I never spoke a word to her, nor, obviously, she to me, but visiting her always brought me a certain solace. In exchange, I'd drop a spare coin into her tin box and leave behind a taper's flame.

In retrospect, I recognize she became a surrogate for Sybil, my lit candle a stand-in for the cut flowers I'd be bringing her each Friday if I were in New York. But I wasn't, was I? I was across the sea, wandering. My weekly visitation to Santa Lucia then, a kind of penance?

One evening, a visiting priest was conducting the mass in Latin, and after lighting my votive I sat down to listen to vespers. I understood absolutely nothing he uttered, yet when the moment came for him to raise the host aloft, an elderly woman nearby whispered "*mistero della fede*" (mystery of faith), and I found myself weeping uncontrollably. Weeping for what I was only then first starting to comprehend about my actions, myself. I recall a sudden desire to receive communion rose within me that evening, yet I refrained. I hadn't earned that rite.

Beneath the rusted cathedral of Iowa's autumn oak, I felt the schoolhouse woods might offer me another kind of catechism. Among its upper rafters flitted a choir of songbirds intoning question after question in cadences I could fairly recognize by then. The prior autumn, not all too long after my initial arrival in Iowa, I'd spotted a notice for bird-watchers on a campus bulletin board and copied down its information. As a city boy I'd known only pigeons and seagulls—bird as nuisance—but the next Sunday, map in hand, I drove to the prescribed rendezvous just past dawn.

I remember the air being cold enough to mist my breath that morning, the surrounding hills already spreading auburn and gold. Recall standing at the edge of a meadow, at the edge of a circle of strangers, not quite sure what to do with my hands.

The answer came quickly though, as palms extended toward me offering a warm thermos and binoculars. Palms that turned into faces, faces into names, and after several more Sundays, into teachers and friends.

At that first gathering I met other mentors, too. Named waxwing and kinglet, teal and wood duck, osprey and egret and cormorant. I learned to focus on treetops and follow flight, to discern wing bars and silhouettes. I heard song patterns separate from the thickets and single cries echo across a still marsh. Hours drifted by as if on a thermal, and soon I forgot who I was, who I'd been. I felt almost as if I'd taken flight from my body, my weight. I stood within a flock watching other flocks, the same southerly wind pulling at the tails of our jackets. It was a Sunday morning like none I'd ever known, a church with no roof, and in the flash of a wingbeat my conversion was complete. I became, a birder.

By the time I arrived at the schoolhouse, I could already delineate subtle markings among the local sparrows and migrating warblers. I recognized the flight patterns of woodpeckers undulating between treetops, of red-tailed hawks climbing ever higher in widening circles. This autumn, however, I found myself paying more attention to the arrow of geese retreating overhead, dividing the sky into seasons, into here and hereafter. Into time, and distances.

3 October. Sybil called again last night. Wanted to see how I felt about her coming out next weekend, since there are cheap seasonal flights.

Said we could meet up in another city nearby, if I'd prefer. St. Louis or Chicago? Part of me got excited, it'd be fun exploring another new town with her. But another part of me can hardly breathe. Here we go again. Wasn't the whole idea of coming out here to start anew? God, this crazy tango of ours. Always one step forward, two steps back ...

5 October. Late afternoon walk along Black Diamond with my new guide for wildflowers. The ditches thick with yellow stick-tights and goldenrod, a few blue beggar's-lice spiking up for contrast. Also spotted the following along the road's shoulder:

  2 Miller Genuine Drafts
  3 squashed snakes and a splotch of frog
  1 Old Milwaukee
  1 Mr. Pibb
  2 partial raccoon skeletons (salvage jaw and a few vertebrae)
  1 wax DeliMart cup—still coated with ants
  1 small brown feather, unidentified

All that on a half-mile stretch. So much left behind and overlooked. So much to take in and record. To save from disappearing...

At the edge of the nearest field stands a long row of round hay bales. Earlis Rohret, the farmer down the road, said their shape is based on Ugandan hut roofs. Supposedly a missionary noticed they'd shed water for up to forty years. Earlis said he laughed at them round balers at first, then went out and bought one. Sure beat stacking square bales into the barn's loft. Plus, the rain only soaks in an inch or so.

Back on the first night of classes, our professor and Writers' Workshop director Frank Conroy drew a simple arc on the blackboard. At one end he wrote an R and at the other end a W, the arc between representing the exchange that happens between Reader and Writer. That exchange, he said, took place at varying points on the curve, depending upon how you wrote your story.

Quickly I'd pulled out my notebook, duly copying his diagram as Conroy then drew an X on the arc that leaned toward the Reader's end. In this case, he went on to explain, you the Writer occupies too large a portion of the arc. You're doing too much work, say your descriptions are so detailed the Reader feels impatient or overwhelmed, or worse yet, condescended to. Not unlike how it feels going out to lunch with someone who's holding forth, not letting you enter the conversation.

Our professor then marked an X on the opposite side of the arc, closer to the Writer's end this time. Now here, Conroy lectured, you the Writer might be asking too much of your Reader. Say, your transitions aren't smooth, or you've arbitrarily changed the story's narrator or point-of-view, or suddenly we're in Oklahoma—so the Reader isn't being sufficiently directed through your tale, or is being asked to fill in too wide or many a gap.

In both cases, Conroy concluded, the Reader pulls out of the story, or dream. So, ideally the point of contact best occurs somewhere midway on the arc, where both parties are bringing similar amounts of energy and imagination to the task of envisioning each story's particulars.

In effect, good storytelling needs to be a co-creation, a dialogue of equal participation. An active and mutual exchange of dreams.

Did Sybil and I have that? A mutual exchange? Were we a good story? One with a clear beginning, middle, and end? A co-creation of dreams, or even horizons? Given the limits of our situation, our plot if you will, was any other destination possible?

I kept thinking about the placement of those Xs on Conroy's arc. About what transpired between Sybil and me. About what got left unsaid on that Lexington Avenue sidewalk. What remained unspoken between us still. Untouched, too. Like those relics in Italy, revered behind glass. Adored, yet from a distance. Was that what I held for Sybil? More adoration than love? Our story more distant than close? Did we keep returning to each other, or keep removing ourselves?

She arrived on a Friday for the long Columbus Day weekend. In the end, we decided to meet in Iowa. My new home was already retreat enough. I picked her up at the airport with flowers in-hand and drove us directly back to the schoolhouse. I felt hesitant, yet also eager to share Redbird Farm's beauty and fortune with someone. With her.

Once home, we fell into each other's arms, fell back into what was most familiar and natural between us. For the first day, we barely descended from the twin bed in the schoolhouse's loft. We reconnected with the landscape of our bodies—our familiar curves and hollows, our skin, our sweat. We indulged each other's languished hungers. We feasted. We slept.

If we spoke, it was only briefly, haltingly. I asked after her sons, who were all grown by now, and we caught up on the handful of her friends I'd met over the years. We talked a bit about my classes at the university, as well as what I was learning from the schoolhouse woods—much of which I found hard to put into tangible words. We returned to what were known quantities, subjects that were safe.

Come morning I took her for a woodswalk, showing her trails that led to the more secluded ponds. It reminded me a little of our early trysts in city parks, back before I'd found my apartment. However, sharing this kind of nature hike in Iowa didn't come so naturally to us. Sybil's quick gait and fashionable clothing seemed out of place in this setting, her speed and style decidedly metropolitan.

Still, we shared what we could of the woods then drove over to nearby Kalona to explore its many antique shops. En route, we passed several Old Order Amish farmsteads on the dirt back roads, and I pulled over so Sybil could take photos of their black buggies and laden clotheslines, their draft horses.

"Oh my, look at that one," she cried. "Isn't she a beauty."

"Yes," I said. "It's a Percheron. They're my favorites, too."

Later that afternoon back at the schoolhouse, Sybil got to try riding one of Andre's horses, swiftly charming him with her verve and laughter. Tina, too, seemed pleased to meet her. Again, Sybil's spirit could seduce most anyone.

On Sunday morning I awoke first and lay listening to her sleeping sighs. I recalled how I often used to read to her in bed. Sybil had introduced me not only to the inspirations of the flesh, but also to some of the very authors whose work spurred me toward trying my hand at prose. Toni Morrison and Gabriel Garcia Marquez. John Edgar Wideman and Jeanette Winterson. Marianne Wiggins. Salman Rushdie. I lay there thinking, would I even be in Iowa if I'd never bumped into Sybil? Across the loft, her clothes draped over the wooden chair before my writing desk. Her blouse chartreuse, not unlike the hue of the jumpsuit she'd worn on the night we first met.

I lay in those sheets beside her, feeling not so much present as tangled up in a moment that had already passed. My hand hovered over her shoulder and a strange, flat feeling I couldn't name descended. Later, I'd confirm it in the dictionary:

> **nostalgia**: (from Greek *nostos*—return home; akin to Old English *genesan*—to survive, or Sanskrit *nasate*—he approaches) **1**: the state of being homesick **2**: a wistful or excessively sentimental sometimes abnormal yearning for return to or of some past period or irrecoverable condition

Before I brought Sybil back to the airport, I showed her the city park where I'd slept in my car those first weeks I landed in Iowa. Hand-in-hand we walked toward the kiddie rides, the merry-go-round not yet closed for the season. We bought tickets and chose our colored horses to ride, and I turned round backwards on mine to snap her picture. The soundtrack spun round with us, all tinny and surreal. Here we are, I thought, another frozen moment, another departure. Here we are, going up and down, round and round. Turning the same old circles.

At the airport gate we hugged, holding on a little longer than usual.

"Well," said Sybil, "we'll talk."

"Yes…" I said, still thinking we'd find a way to say what we couldn't, that I'd find the right words.

At first it was almost indiscernible—a bare break in the brush alongside the trail, a parting of branches yielding an arbor of entry, the leaves underfoot looking disturbed, their undersides slightly darker. And if you squinted, you'd note how that darkness drew forward into a thin line, threading through the trunks and brambles. Follow that line and eventually you'd spot two small indentations in the dirt, sharp and precise, twin crescents. A step further and there'd be another pair, then another. The ground trod with deer tracks—silent, yet suggesting a trajectory.

Following these deer runs, I soon realized they covered distances far more swiftly than the schoolhouse woods' main trails—bisecting nearly every angle and ridge of Redbird Farm, hopping over run-off creeks, ducking thorn bushes, barely pausing before vaulting neighboring fences. Further tracking taught me to discern between a deer's slow walk and a trot; how hoof-prints splayed more when running; how in soft mud their dewclaws showed. And after measuring the prints I learned a deer's back feet were actually smaller than their front ones, which

I guess made sense considering how they bounded—leaps that could exceed seven feet. I even dug one fine specimen from the dried floodplain and set it on my nightstand as a paperweight.

I took note of other commuters, too. The wide lumbering prints of raccoon, the opossum's disjointed rear thumb, the smooth swath of muskrat sliding down a pond's bank. With the help of a library book, I similarly began studying the scat each left behind, too. Deer pellets had an almost olive hue, looking like large capers but smelling more like mushrooms. The wild turkey's was a round dollop topped with an off-white powder. Coyote turds were a rarer find, similar in size and shape to a dog's yet laced with their preys' fur. Sometimes I couldn't believe I was eagerly poking sticks at piles of feces, was literally walking around cradling a guide to shit under my elbow.

Emerging from a deer run one morning, I ran into Tina on the main trail. She saw the guidebook in my hand and shook her head.

"You know," she said after a few steps, "there are other things animals feel compelled to do."

I stared at her, clueless.

"Haven't you noticed the scrapes?"

"No," I said, "what's a scrape?"

She led me down the main trail to the fork between the Woods and Lower Ponds near the rowboat, where a patch of dried leaves had been pawed clear.

"Some kind of territorial marker?" I asked.

"Well, yes," she said. "It's rutting season. A buck will come and tend this each day, leaving behind his scent for a doe. They tend to sniff one another out before committing to anything...Not too unlike people."

She waited, as if fishing for a response. I could tell she was curious about the precise nature of my long-distance relationship with Sybil, yet knew she'd never ask directly. Just like I'd never ask her why she was living alone. I knelt down, ran my fingers over the fresh ground, and brought them to my nose. I didn't smell anything.

"And then there's this," said Tina, pointing to a snapped branch overhead. She reached out and touched its edges.

"What's that?"

"Bucks have glands near their eyes that they rub. See how high this is above the ground?"

"Uh-huh."

"That's a warning signal to other smaller bucks. They're all rubbing their antlers now, too, preparing for battle. Only the fittest get to mate."

Something clicked in my head. I'd been noticing several sapling trunks stripped of bark along the runs, yet hadn't made the connection. Tina glanced at the ground, then back up to the broken branch.

"This one seems to be a fairly big one. He'll do just fine."

Her gaze seemed to be shaping the actual buck out of thin air, forming the curves and points of its rack, its sloping neck and rear haunches. After a moment she blinked, and looked back toward me and my beginner's guidebook.

"Well, carry on," she said, and walked away.

I retraced my steps into the woods and followed a run until I found a rubbed tree trunk. Its exposed flesh felt cool and smooth, sticky. Further on lay a second and third such signpost, and I fingered each frayed strand of bark as if for Braille. At my next footstep, a sudden tremor burst in the brush ahead—a retreating flash of brown and darting white tail, leaping up and over the ridge, gone. I caught my breath, and on a small knoll nearby found the spot where the doe had been bedding, the leaves flattened but not scraped. Beneath my palm, the ground was still warm. I curled my body into the spare space, drawing my knees to my chest. I closed my eyes.

Soon it felt as if another whole dimension to the woods unfurled. In the dry leaves beneath my head I could hear the tiny footsteps of insects, then a nearby creek trickling toward Lower Pond. The sound of moving water conjured up more memories of Venice. A week prior to my finally leaving there, Alessandro showed up with a borrowed motorboat. As my going away gift, he took us out puttering among the more remote islets of the lagoon, all the while recounting their histories and folklore. Tall tales of one's stone ruins where great galleons once pulled in their sails for customs. Or of another named after Lazarus, where Lord Byron sought refuge in his final days. Old outposts now abandoned to all but the exiles of psychiatric hospitals, or lone fishermen tending to their nets, or dank monks to their ritual prayers and letterpresses.

Aless then steered us toward Venice proper and cut the engine, paddled us into her thin canals. We drifted past back entrances to the *palazzi* and alongside small docks where the dead were once piled high during the plague. Aless searched out dark doorways where opera divas slipped away from their adoring fans, then pointed out how the steps on the Rialto bridge were carved low so women descending in gowns would appear to be floating on air. And suddenly that's how I felt too, as if an entirely different city had magically floated up to the surface before me. Venice as she was meant to be explored, by water and oar. Up close and personal.

A similar sensation once struck me in Manhattan—one New Year's Eve when Sybil and I splurged on a helicopter ride over the city. A last minute idea, we literally ran out onto the flight pad along the East River and climbed aboard. I remember how elegant she looked that evening, her hair gelled and pulled back in a French braid, her profile backlit by skyscrapers. I'd dressed up too, in a suit jacket for once, and as we awaited liftoff I was thinking how romantic this felt. Thinking, I could do this forever. Stay with her forever.

I caught her eye. Between us, I could feel her breath.

"Nice, huh?" I said.

Sybil smiled and reached for my hand. Words seemed superfluous and yet I found myself searching for them.

Then a pair of tourists hopped aboard and strapped themselves in across from us. The door was swung and latched shut, and in the next breath we were aloft, rising over Midtown. The young Japanese couple was beside themselves, all giddy and clicking away photographs. And who could blame them, what better way to see the city of skyscrapers than from above? On their fingers I glimpsed shiny wedding bands. Newlyweds, I figured.

Again I glanced Sybil's way, and for the briefest moment wondered what the newlyweds made of us. Did they think we were married?

"Oh, look," said Sybil, and pulled me closer to her window.

Below us the crowds were already gathering in Times Square, all the lights in the theater district twinkling. Later we'd catch a play and eat at our favorite restaurant on 45th Street, then rush up to Central Park for the midnight fireworks. Just like we'd done last New Year's Eve. And the New Year's Eve before that.

And would do again, the following year. We had our rituals, select annual celebrations we could rely on sharing, and yet I recognized no new resolutions were waiting for us back at the landing pad. No future proposals or vows or even short-term projections. Only this hovering cusp of the present. This safe and warm holding pattern of ours.

The chopper lurched higher, its engine whining, the ground spiraling away. Gravity pulled at my stomach as we veered south, shadowing Broadway down past the Village and

The New School, past Chinatown and another of our favorite restaurants. Was that all we ever did—eat and go to shows and make love? I clasped Sybil's hand but the gesture felt empty, confused. Ahead of us loomed the glowing crown of the Woolworth Building, baroque as any wedding cake. Mocking us. I blinked in dismay. Pressed down the queasiness rising in my throat, that bottomless fear we both felt too terrified to name aloud.

I bolted upright in my Iowa deer's bed, gasping and dizzy. Apart from the surrounding woods nothing much had changed, had it? The two of us were still hanging on in midair. Still spiraling round on our merry-go-round of denials. What was wrong with me? Other people managed these kinds of transitions. Other people moved on with their lives, chose a career, settled down. Clearly this vertigo wasn't only about my letting go of Sybil, but something older and deeper and still illegible to me.

16 October. 6:30 AM woodswalk. Some mornings can seem so perfect out here. Like for a moment you've glimpsed the very dawn on its perch. A touch of Eden. Then you'll come upon a hillside of wilted nightshade berries, half-drowned by last night's rain. Ants scrambling to restore their caved-in colony. An old apple lying in the dirt, half-bitten and brown. Paradise lost . . .

Hardly wrote anything this past week. Too distracted, or rattled . . . Late last night the phone rang again, but I didn't dare answer. Literally backed myself up against the wall.

"You need to insulate," said Tina.

"Huh?"

"For the cold. It's coming."

"Oh, right," I said.

With winter right around the bend, Tina helped me draw up a punch list of preparations. My first chore was to clean and install all the schoolhouse's storm windows. Next came laying a thick berm of earth and hay around the water pump alongside the barn downhill, and double-checking its backup space heater. The schoolhouse's propane tank gauge read ninety percent full, my car's radiator fluid good to -40°. I bought myself a better set of used tires and a brand new battery. All that remained on my list: Strip away ivy from around the chimney hood. Gather kindling. Cut firewood.

Tina lent me her chainsaw and I perused its user's manual from cover to cover. A week went by, then another before her son Philip came out from town to cut an ample supply for his own woodstove. He wasn't much older than I was, but a real woodsman and hunter who regularly wrote articles for outdoorsmen magazines. He pulled up his truck to the schoolhouse and pointed at the chainsaw still sitting on my porch deck.

"So, you ever use one of those before?"

"No," I said, and looked to the ground.

He gave me a crash course in its choke and brake, and how to periodically tighten down on the chain—part of which I remembered from reading the manual.

"Do its teeth need filing?" I offered.

"No, they're fine," he said, and pulled sharply on its chord. After three tries the engine screamed. Philip pushed in its choke, adjusted the idle, then shut it down.

"Okay. Now you try," he said, and stepped back.

I bent over and went through the same paces, but at best could only manage a sputter. After about the twentieth try, I looked up at Philip.

"Well," he said, "how about if I cut and you stack."

"Perfect," I said, and hopped into his truck's cab.

We drove into the woods toward deadfall Philip had already scouted—seasoned elm he said burned hot, hickory and oak a little slower, and mulberry that split well though tended to leave more ash than flame. He backed up the Dodge as close to a downed trunk as possible and within minutes the woods whined with our violence. Between carrying armloads of logs to the truck, I watched the way Philip first carved a notch from below the trunks, meting out lengths that would fit his stove. I studied where he placed his feet and how he never seemed to force the saw, using gravity to his advantage. Here was someone who knew what to do with his hands, who could clearly fend for himself, his wife, and two sons. Catching me staring, he lowered the idle.

"You see this lever here?" he yelled.

"Yeah."

"You have to depress it every now and again. Oils the chain."

"Right," I said.

He kicked at a log until it rolled, then continued cutting. There was no fat on any of his movements, no extra energy expended, no time wasted. He didn't bother with thinking about what he was doing, he just acted. He cut things apart, quickly and cleanly. Soon the truck bed was filled and Philip gathered our jackets. Once inside the cab, he pulled out his earplugs and tossed them onto the dashboard.

"Those would be a good thing to get," he said.

"What?!" I said.

He smiled and steered the Dodge around a bend in the trail. Passing branches scraped at both our windows. I could smell fresh cut wood on my clothes.

"So, you liking it out here?" asked Philip.

"Yeah, it's heaven ... All this solitude."

He leveled his gaze at me then smiled again, this time more wryly.

"Yeah well, wait 'til winter," he said.

"Why's that?"

"You'll see."

22 October. Sitting here before the fireplace, the whole room flickering with shadows and flame. My back is killing me, but it feels good to have split the wood by myself. Philip left me with an extra axe, wedge, and maul. Guess he figured the worst I could do is lose a toe or two ... Or maybe amputation is precisely what's required here. Cutting things off quick and clean? In one fell swoop, once and for all? Yeah, right. Easier written than done ... I ought to get up and give Alessandro a call. Check in on how he's doing. This couch feels too good, though. Dolce Far Niente.

Doing nothing, I was learning, wasn't only sweet but also easier to swallow. Like usual, I was choosing the lesser path. I knew Sybil and I were fated to part, I just couldn't see my way clear as to *when* or *where* or *how* that could ever happen. Most days, I couldn't even understand the *why*.

At the university, too, our weekly workshops were proving ever more taxing emotionally. It was time to start proposing our thesis projects, and you could practically taste the vulnerability in the air. Sharing our works-in-progress felt more loaded now, the stakes and consequences suddenly sky high.

One evening a classmate literally fainted, mostly due to two anxious days prior without sleep or food. Still, Conroy's teaching philosophy remained cut and dry—the text itself held pre-eminence in our group critiques, not any of our subjective feelings or responses. He repeatedly focused us back to our drafts at-hand, the way our words linked up on the page. Readers only received the manuscript before them, not our lofty intentions. Meaning had to emerge from the printed words alone, via the clarity of our language and phrasing, the conscious spaces we left between our sentences. What one both did and didn't say were equally relevant.

Personally, I struggled most with clarity and with completing my drafts. No big surprise there, I guess, but a few classmates also reported feeling "distant" from my characters.

Citing a certain "remove" in my writing. I felt frustrated, my words failing me. It got to the point where returning to the sanctuary of the schoolhouse came as a welcome relief. There, I didn't have to talk or face up to anyone.

Instead, I picked up my regimen of woodswalks, my documenting of days. By now the wild asters had withered away, leaving mostly lobelia with their bottom blue petals pouting. Several trails had turned spongy and at spots slippery, fungi fanning out along fallen boughs—oyster and honey mushrooms and unidentified little pear-shaped balls that spread their spores in tiny puffs of green smoke. I parked myself on a dry stump with my journal and tried to catch up on all the autumn changes I'd been missing. Clearly I still wasn't being observant enough, wasn't looking or getting close enough to my subject matter.

When next I glanced up, a pair of chipmunks was chasing one another nearby. They jumped onto a tree trunk less than three feet away, so close I could study how their tiny claws clamped onto the bark, the way their tails kept adjusting for better balance. And suddenly it occurred to me—if I just stopped stumbling about, then nature would eventually come to me. In the days that followed, I quickly found this to be true. Insects came first, then other small animals. Some approached depending on how long I'd sat, others on how still. And others unconsciously, because I'd finally woven myself into the tapestry.

It was almost as if I had to unlearn everything in order to learn anew. Go back to a time before books and words meant anything to me, before I was even taught to color within the lines. Back before definitions. And the more I thought about this the more sense it made. With my head always buried in this or that field guide, how was I ever going to glean or forge a new path out here on my own? Forget about reading guidebooks and covering ground, if I really wanted to embrace the wisdom of the woods then I needed to cultivate the patience of trees. Only there and then, I figured, might I truly grow.

With this new approach in mind, I awoke the next day before dawn and hiked deep into the woods. I propped myself between two elms overlooking a draw, and waited. Slowly, the coming light licked at the sky until a touch past sunrise, when a lone doe came prancing down the draw's thin run. I held my breath as she advanced, closer and still closer. Finally she sensed me and pulled up dead in her tracks. I recalled an article on lion taming I'd once read that said the tamer's whip and pistol and chair were all mere show. The real mediator was the space between man and beast. There was a distance from which a lion or tiger will opt to turn and run, a point where it'll freeze, and a proximity from which it must attack. Critical distances that could be measured to the centimeter.

The doe and I stood motionless, locked in each other's stare. Distant, and yet linked. Her breaths were like mine, short and sharp, pushing out sideways from flared nostrils. Her ears cupped wide, her tail lowered. Once or twice she stamped a fore hoof in warning, equally vigilant of me, ready for the barest twitch of my hand or legs. Our conversation must have lasted only a minute or two, perhaps less, yet felt like hours of intimate exchange. Finally, she dipped her head, pivoted, and quietly trotted off for cover. I stood on transfixed, feeling more naked than elated. Literally trembling.

Meanwhile, back on the schoolhouse's stone table lay the open dictionary, its binding still split to the same page with yet another intransitive definition for communicate—to open into each other.

Anatomy

✳

My brother was born with a broken heart. Literally. A hole down its center, the pulmonary veins and arteries transposed and twisted on themselves—its beating irregular, choked. If such a heart were found in a newborn today or even ten years later, it could have been mended through surgery. In 1958, however, there was nothing to be done. Nothing but wait out seven long months till mercy.

I never met him. He came and went before I was born. I didn't even learn about him until I was nearly eleven, when my mother sat me down at the kitchen table one evening. No wait, we were already sitting. Dinner was finished and we were about to drink our tea. Just another typical night around the house, with my mother sitting opposite me and my older sister off to my left. I can't seem to place my father, though. Probably he was already downstairs in the basement tinkering with broken televisions, a side job of his that helped make ends meet. Somehow I remember carrots, too. Cubed carrots, the kind that came in a can. Perhaps they still sat at the edge of my plate, pushed aside and cold.

My mother paused before speaking. I remember that, too. The way she slid the tag from the tea bag between her teeth like a toothpick. The way her words came out, slow and deliberate. Choked back even, once or twice. My sister, who was surely old enough to remember it all, sat dutifully silent, her eyes not daring to meet mine. Of the exact conversation concerning our brother, however, I recall very little: that he was born with a full head of hair, that he slept in an oxygen tent, and that the box he was buried in was very, very small—more like the size of something you'd expect to put in the ground to grow.

I can't say why my family waited so long to tell me, or why they finally did that evening. No doubt they had their reasons, their scars. Yet at the time, as a child, I remember feeling very confused, betrayed. Not necessarily because I was denied a brother, but because I was denied the knowing. That certain stories had been withheld from me. Secrets in the dark I couldn't know nor comprehend. Absences. Shadows. The world suddenly felt unfamiliar to me that evening. A place I couldn't entirely trust at face value anymore.

At public school, I started to second-guess what was being told to me by my teachers and textbooks, too. Started revisiting all those countless facts and figures—1492, long division, mitochondria, the Boston Tea Party. Started dissecting my test papers' red ink for hidden clues and connections. Yet all I could decipher was that each textbook was being treated as a separate subject, a separate discipline, and ultimately the only discipline we learned was how to answer, not how to question. Not how to reason or at least search for reasons. Reasons why the earth wasn't the center of the universe. Why history would again and again repeat itself. Why one son would die while the other remained.

30 October. Dawn. 6:30 AM and I blew it. Was supposed to meet Philip before sunrise. He's probably deep in the cattails with his cousin by now, all camouflaged and watching the skies. Their hands and fingers poised. Meanwhile, here you are, kneeling in the grass at the marsh's edge, feeling like some schoolboy. The one who doesn't get picked for the team yet still has to sit on the sidelines and watch. You overslept?! What an asshole!!! Okay, forget it. Let it go. Just sit here and try to learn something. Watch and record . . .

A thin mist hung over the marsh, the sky a dull grey yet growing brighter by the minute. All was quiet, waiting for sunrise. For movement. I squatted in the duckweed, shifting my weight yet trying to minimize my boots' loud sucking in the mud. To the south a barred owl called, still clinging to the last of night.

My left calf started to cramp and I rubbed it to keep the blood flowing. What was I doing here? I didn't believe in any of this—in guns or killing, in eating meat even. I should go home, back to my books and breakfast. Back to my warm, dry bed.

Then, a shot rang out. I looked up at an approaching wedge of ducks breaking formation over the water. Two more shots blasted, dropping one of the drakes. The rest veered toward me, the whistle of one's wings close enough to distinguish, their collective whir pulling against the sky to get out of range. Behind me, a sudden splashing, then words. "Come. Give it. Give it here, boy." The air seemed heavy with echoes, with heartbeats thumping against my ribs.

As a young boy, I'd had the typical encounters with slingshots and BB guns you might expect. Shooting at tin cans and bottles, stop signs and street lights. My only experience with what I might call close to hunting, however, came on a playground. I was twelve, thirteen at most, and playing paddleball. During one game, the ball was hit off the court and rolled a good distance away. One of my friends went to retrieve it, and after a moment called us over excitedly. He'd found a small bat out in broad daylight, dangling from the park's chain link fence. It was sleeping, its little wings folded around its head.

I don't quite recall what happened next. All I remember is that suddenly a bloodied bat was lying on the asphalt and four of us standing around with paddles in our hands. To this day I can't say for sure whether or not I swung, though ultimately it doesn't matter. Even if I didn't, I didn't stop the killing. What does matter, is I've entirely blocked out the moment, have handily blanked out all personal culpability.

Squatting among Redbird Farm's cold marsh reeds, I heard breaches being broken nearby. The rising sun cleared the tree line and the marsh's mist slowly dissipated. An oarlock creaked and then came a voice, Philip's, calling me by name. As if I was complicit, which I guess was true. For I had to admit that beyond merely standing by while the guns blared, I had also felt a more than faint physical anticipation within my own chest. My own fingertips.

3 AM. The 6th, no 7th of November. Waking from dreams. Sweating. Outside the schoolhouse, nothing. Not even moonlight. Silence thick as blankets, then another screech. Long and piercing, finally muffled back into the night. An infant's cry? A rabbit's howl? Nearby the clock ticks and the room slowly returns... windows, walls, ceiling... sleet tapping against the rooftop... the faint moaning of diesels on the interstate, three miles distant... Go back to sleep. It was nothing... just owls working third shift... nothing...

The schoolhouse woods proved home to varied owls, or hushwings, as I'd learned some Native Americans called them. They'd become one of my favorite birds, in part because they seemed so mysterious and unattainable. Their feather tips sworn to whispers, their great wingspans not so much fighting gravity as caressing the winds to conjure flight. Bird of omens, bird of night. They seemed to the dark sky what sharks were to deep water. Solitary and insatiable. Fate's swift and silent hand.

Every night I'd hear their garbled hoots. Or on some nights, only the startled squeals of their prey. Sometimes a barred owl's measured croons could lull me to sleep. Or sometimes I'd crawl out from under my sheets and into the night to stalk them myself. I'd crouch along the dark hillsides and cup my ears trying to fix on their positions. Shine my flashlight into bough after empty bough. Sing harmony with their hoots, trying to coax one in. Once I swear something whisked by my head, but it could just as well have been a sudden breeze, or bat. Or angel. At four in the morning many strange things are a-wing, many prayers left unanswered.

Time and again I'd head back toward the schoolhouse crestfallen and empty-handed. The only tangible signs of the owls I'd muster were the grey oblong pellets they'd cough up and leave behind. Like a tease I'd find those by the dozen, long-dried and littering the ground beneath favored roosts. But the hunter itself, never.

Back indoors, I'd turn on the schoolhouse lights and lay out these pellets side by side on the stone tabletop. Carefully I'd dissect each one, extracting tiny vertebrae and rodent jaws from the matted fur, as if trying to puzzle something back together. Precisely what, I didn't know, but I kept at it, almost obsessively. Sorting and storing each victim's remains in small glass jars, not unlike the reliquaries I'd seen in Venice. Pieces, but no whole. Evidence without any conviction. By the time I'd finish, the next dawn would already be slanting through the schoolhouse door. I'd climb back to the perch of my loft bed and sleep well into the day.

Soon, my whole constitution seemed bent on understanding this intricate dance between prey and predator, between stalking and survival. I could feel it becoming my new obsession. I started missing classes at the university, and the schoolhouse started to resemble some taxonomist's nightmare. Every free surface, littered with objects I'd stumble upon during my daily woodswalks—fallen feathers, seedpods, and nibbled black walnuts. Antlers and eggshells, sumac and loam. A series of unearthed paw prints padded across one windowsill like a tiny parade. My walls, haphazardly adorned with dried cattails and teasel, shed snakeskins and the spent husks of dragonfly nymphs.

Somewhere in all those objects there had to be some ulterior design. Some natural explanation beneath what remained and what didn't. Some answer for why Sybil and I couldn't just part ways. The question was literally gnawing away at me from inside.

12 November. Creek beds frozen over this morning. One tree listing against another overhead, creaking like a moored ship. Clocks turned back now. The whole country trying to spare itself from the dark.

... For I am the King of Owls.
Where I float no shadow falls.
I have hungers, such terrible hungers, you cannot know.
Lords, I sharpen my talons on your bones.   —Louise Erdrich

Wondering about my own hunger. Never been "terribly" hungry myself, yet always able to eat. And what might that mean, not quite ambitious enough? Lacking the killer instinct? The requisite nerve or desire? Hungry for hunger, then? So then, where's the true seat of hunger, in the stomach or the heart?

Never made the connection before, but wondering if my heart's malformed, too? Maybe it physiologically can't let go.

14 November. In Workshop tonight, thinking how our process often feels like a medical consultation. All of us sitting round a large wooden table with our stories before us like patients on the slab, offering up diagnoses as to what's "wrong" or needs "fixing." A palpable chill in the room. Our language turning almost surgical: "Cut this out" or "Excise that" or as one classmate said, "Go ahead, tear me apart."

A few days into deer hunting season, there came a knock on the schoolhouse's front door, the first ever in fact. Philip's cousin Sean stood on the deck. The curve of a hunting bow hung from his fist.

"I just took a buck," he said, "Tina thought you might want to watch me field dress it."

Did I, really? I wasn't sure, but slid on my boots and followed him onto the wooded trail. As we walked I asked questions about his compound bow to cover my nerves. Sean assured me all its pulleys and sightings mostly helped lessen the number of deer wounded, and that for him bow hunting was still far more spiritual than shotgun. Closer to the prey, to the Native American concept of the animal offering itself to you.

On the ground I started to notice brick-red stains every three paces.

"Arterial blood," said Sean, "from the jugular. It was a risky shot, but I had it."

He then told me heart's blood was darker still, and lung shot typically brighter and frothy. The dotted trail veered into the brush, but we stayed on the open path and soon spotted a bright yellow quill hanging in naked branches. Sean grabbed this marker and we ducked into the woods. Beyond the next set of brambles lay a slight clearing, and at its far edge, the downed deer.

He was young, a "button buck," his long neck curled back like a swan's, his forelegs crossed just above the dewclaws. Graceful even now, I thought, even with an arrow's gash in its throat. Beside me Sean stood very still, then kneeled and rocked the deer onto its back, drawing a squat knife down the length of its abdomen. I flinched, but didn't bolt.

He narrated the entire procedure for me, his words matching his hands' movements as he first carved around the anus to free the bowels then methodically separated the kidneys, liver, and heart for keeping. One slit to the diaphragm, another to loosen the bladder, and all the other innards slid out. I was surprised at how swift the process was, how multicolored the organs. How my own stomach hadn't rebelled. Finally, Sean tilted the cavity and the remaining blood spilled. Gallons it seemed, slow to seep away. Wisps of steam rose from the ground. Sean didn't ask for any help carrying the carcass, and I didn't offer. I forgot to ask him why he'd kept the heart.

When I got back to the schoolhouse the telephone was ringing, Tina asking if I was ready to go to the funeral. For a moment I stood confused then remembered the other recent death—a local woman named Paige Walters, who used to live in Tina's house and raise sheep in the schoolhouse's pastures. While I'd never personally met Paige, I had crossed paths with her son Jim, a local expert on bluebirds who was helping conserve their numbers in the area. As it turned out, he'd also been one of the last children to attend classes at the schoolhouse before it closed down.

Tina drove us toward town, saying little. Still, I could sense she was pleased I'd offered to accompany her. The funeral parlor was on the far side of Iowa City, its parking lot nearly full when we arrived. Inside, Jim and his father looked cramped in their suits and ties, yet greeted us warmly. I shook hands then stepped aside. Organ music sifted in from the chapel.

The reverend began with standards, Psalms and Ecclesiastes, invoking John the Good Shepherd and the Bible's claim to more than one hundred references to sheep. My focus drifted over to the casket, which was flanked by yellow mums and pink gladiola. I could see the fall of hair on Paige's forehead, the fold of her spotted wrists. The lower portion of the casket was closed, looking like half-drawn linens, a bible opened at her waist. Her reading glasses were also in place, a detail that struck me as odd and unsettling. Once the opening notes to "How

Great Thou Art" rose, Tina shared her hymnal and we all sang along.

Jim and his sister then took turns at the podium. They spoke of the diary their mother kept on the kitchen shelf, thick with notes on her sheep and garden and family:

'July 19, 1963 - Jim bought me a hose to water my flowers, dear boy.'

'July 6, 1964 - Julie spilled hot soup on her face, the poor thing. I love her so.'

'Dec 17, 1965 - Dad passed away today.'

'Dec 22, 1965 - My husband gave me a new coat for Christmas, early.'

Slowly, I began to envision the well-worn path to the barn, the flashlight held tightly through the long nights of lambing, the wooden stable and its peace—a place she'd come to call *'the most natural place for Christ to be born.'*

"She was a farmer," said Jim, and then added nothing.

Outside, neighbors lingered while buttoning coats, and a little girl in a lace and velvet dress strayed onto the funeral parlor's lawn. She held a makeshift spyglass rolled from the 23rd Psalm to her eye, scanning the treetops.

Tina didn't want to attend the actual burial and I wondered why. I wondered more about her ex-husband and family too, but on the drive home we again kept silent. Finally I asked an idle question about lambs, and she shared how Paige had been ailing for seventeen years, and that this past summer had thrown herself a "going away" party. How in recent months she'd been freezing individual suppers for her husband, enough to last him through the coming winter and well into the new year.

Soon the last traffic lights below town gave way to open farmland. Ahead, I spotted the glint of a combine, advancing along the edge of dried stalks.

"You know," said Tina. "You never truly belong to a place until you bury one of your dead there."

I glanced her way, but she was staring out the windshield.

Back at the schoolhouse, I paced about from the windows to the walls. I climbed up to my loft bed and tried to nap but the last thing Tina said had unnerved me. I changed my clothes and re-entered the woods.

After heading down into the draw below Sean's deer stand, I circled upwind until I again found signs of blood. He'd told me a shot deer typically bolts for a good hundred to two hundred feet, then stands still, unsure of what's happened to it. I followed the trail halfway up the next ridge to where this seemed true, the puddle of blood wider. To me, it sure looked dark enough to be from the heart. I tried to imagine the young buck pausing and looking back to the place where it had just been, trying to remember something.

On the ground, the red splotches led from one to the next. They climbed a second ridge and broke out onto the muddied path among my daily footprints, then ducked back into the brush. My shoulders rounded as I tracked through deep and deeper thickets, panting and on all fours now, imagining the injured animal's heaving chest, its choices growing more erratic, its movements more and more clumsy until the hard ground came up, stiff and stained. I studied the dirt's scramble of leaves and hooves, dragging on for another ten feet, then the final mound of entrails. Since morning, other scavengers had come too, the deer's stomach torn open and revealing a well-fed mulch of green. Their guilty tracks receded into the brush.

I knew how I'd always felt about hunting, and what I knew now hadn't changed it all that much. Was it violent? Yes. Was it necessary? No. And yet, the case wasn't so simply put. I knew other things now as well. Not only about Iowa's strict hunting seasons and fees and licensing limits, but of Sean's weeks of watching scrapes and runs and patterns. Of his dawns in the deer stand waiting breathless, not only for an encounter, but an accountability. Of waiting still, upwards of an hour, to give the prey the privacy of its own death. Of how nothing gets shrink-wrapped for supermarkets, and nothing goes to waste. Of a winter's worth of venison left at a country preacher's door, who'll feed on it Saturday and stand up Sunday to preach of joys shared and quiet sufferings. Of heretofore unseen and unknown intimacies, not unlike those hand-wrapped and waiting within a farmer's freezer door.

Yet there was still something I couldn't quite reconcile for myself, and not only about hunting. Sure, I could accept the whole prey/predator dynamic, the fact that nothing in nature lived unless something else died. I could dissect that argument and swallow it whole. But it still didn't explain why I'd been the brother who survived, or why Sybil and I couldn't. Why I didn't seem to have the heart to face any endings or responsibility in my life.

I'd always thought I'd had heart. Thought it was what helped make me sensitive enough to want to be a writer in the first place. You needed to have compassion for your characters, after all. Needed to get inside their heads and their shoes, their hesitations, their failings.

Heart, too, underscored my initial attraction to Sybil. It wasn't only her vivacious beauty that drew me close, but something deeper. That first night at the Kiev restaurant we did talk a little about her fractured marriage, and beneath her words I could hear the faint tremor of disappointment and injury, a hurt and confusion I recognized immediately. Kindness, above all else, was what we needed at our table. And affirmation. And thankfully, we somehow found one another that night. We were both of us, broken birds.

One night after Workshop I joined a couple of classmates for a beer. It was well past midnight by the time I left the bar, the streets slick with rainfall. By the time I veered onto Black Diamond Road I could feel myself slowly dozing at the wheel. I opened the windows wide despite the rain, turned up the radio.

"Keep it between the ditches," I told myself. "Between the ditches."

About a mile and a half from home and by then barely squinting, I glimpsed something lying in the road. A raccoon or opossum I thought, and pulled over to make certain it wasn't injured. What I found in the cast of my headlights, however, was a great horned owl. It lay partly on its side, the tufts on its crown wet and half plastered, its neck limp.

In the distance a dog began barking. I felt strangely jumpy, guilty almost, as if in my stupor I'd been the one who struck the bird. I stared down at it for a long time, then leaned over and folded in an errant wing. By then the rain had stilled, moonlight sifting between the clouds overhead, dark shadows stretching toward me from the near tree line. I stood stockstill in the middle of the road, my lungs clutching for air. My shoulders, shivering.

Finally, I reached down and lifted the owl from the wet pavement. The first thing that struck me was the softness of its feathers. Then its weight registered on the tips of my fingers, seemingly too heavy for flight. I cradled it before me, a sliver of moon reflecting off its curved beak. I took a step, then another. When I reached the road's edge, however, I didn't lay the carcass on the gravel shoulder. Instead, I swiftly opened my car's trunk and cleared a space alongside the spare tire and jumper cables.

Addendum: Bubo Virginianus—Great Horned Owl. Also known as Cat Owl, Big Hoot Owl, Le Grand-Duc, Tecolote Cornudo, Tiger of the Sky. Easily identified by crowning "ear" tufts. Also yellow eyes, dark beak, white throated bib while perching. Wingspan - up to 59 inches. Average weight - Male 3.3 lbs. Female 3.7 lbs. Call - soft and dovelike, 3–5 syllables commonly strung together. Prey - everything from crayfish to copperheads, scorpion to woodchuck, but prefers rodents and rabbits. Range – from western Alaska across Canada, south throughout the Americas down to Tierra del Fuego. Highly adaptable, aggressive and secretive. Only significant population decline due to indiscriminate shootings, habitat depletion, and roadkill.

"I've got a great horned," I said to Chris on the phone, "found it on the road last night. Can you help me?"

Chris was one of the first friends I'd made in Iowa. He'd already graduated from the Workshop and lived alongside the river south of town. Originally from eastern Kentucky, he was no novice to the woods. He'd known people there who actually ate owl during the Depression to survive. I figured he'd know how to save its pelt.

"Sure, bring it over tomorrow or Tuesday. I'll show you how," he said.

"Great!"

"Oh, and don't tell anyone."

"Why?" I asked.

"Just don't."

For three days I drove around with a dead owl nestled in a cooler of ice on the backseat of my car. It lay quietly and unseen, waiting in parking lots outside the English department, the grocery store, the post office. Waiting for Chris. At the time his wife was eight months pregnant with their second child and experiencing early contractions, so he was suddenly busy running around to doctors and pharmacies. Meanwhile, I went to the library and hovered around the nature stacks, poring over any book on owls I could find. In one volume, a two page spread of stop-action photography showed their exact killing sequence: the bird's feet coiled way back; the sudden rise of its shoulders; the talons thrust forward; the eyes blinking on impact; the beak twisting; the swallowing, whole.

I also learned why Chris told me to keep quiet. Strict regulations and fines were levied for possession—$1000 for any owl or part thereof. Talons, pelt, even a single feather. I told myself what I was doing, however, was justified. My motives were sound. Something so full of life shouldn't be allowed to simply rot at roadside, right? I was going to preserve the pelt not possess it, I told myself. I was neither prey nor predator, but preserver.

On the fourth day I replaced the cooler's melted ice with a fresh bag and that evening was able to reach Chris on the phone.

"Look," he said, "I'm too crazy right now and you can't afford to wait much longer. Why don't you just do it yourself?"

I felt my palm on the receiver.

"Okay?" I said.

"Start at the feet. Make two cuts, then work your way up, slow and steady. Leave yourself enough time, though. It's going to take a few hours."

The next morning was cool and a little windy. I set up two sawhorses and several old fence planks downwind of the schoolhouse and spread newspapers across their surface. I then lay out whatever sharp "operating" tools I could scrounge: my pocket knife, an exacto, a pair of scissors, wire cutters. Lastly, I placed a chair with its back to the breeze then leaned forward and held my breath while taking off the cooler's cover. My fingers balked against the cold plastic bag, then grasped their prey—the feathered weight airborne once again.

As I lay the bird on the tabletop, however, a heaviness crept over me. The owl's head hung awkwardly to the side, its eyes closed, talons stiff and curled inward. Gone was its regal stance and halting gaze, the Grand Duke dethroned, defenseless. I sighed, doubting myself. Why the hell was I doing this? Then I noted the sunlight playing on its feathers: speckled and mottled and striped, tawny and mud, pearl and umber. I spread out the perfect fan of one wing, thinking: No, this is far too beautiful to leave to the maggots, to just let pass into dust. I had to save it somehow. I took up the knife and gingerly pressed it against the bird's right knee.

The blade slid into the skin without resistance. No response erupted from the feathered mound, no dark blood. I exhaled, then reminded myself to inhale. Slowly I guided the blade around the circumference of its leg. What was it Chris said? Massage the skin's membrane away from the muscle and peel back, massage and peel. I leaned over the owl, pinched the skin between my fingertips, and gave a tiny tug.

It yielded.

Soon I could slip a finger underneath. At first touch, the meat of the thigh felt cool and a little clammy. I imagined my fingerprints tacking to its surface. Should I have worn gloves? My breaths were coming shorter, faster. I freed the skin surrounding the other leg and instinctively reached for the scissors, watching myself slice between the two leg flaps as if from a great height. Now exposing a curved thigh, the color of young grapes. Now tiny highways of veins, still holding blood. Now probing and clawing my way toward the belly. A cloud hovered before the sun, covering me in shadow.

I drew a forearm across my sweating brow. "Slow down, slow down," I told myself. "Easy does it."

But weeks of sifting through abandoned pellets had left me sorely unsated. Some part of me needed to witness the dark inner workings of a true predator, to touch that kind of hunger. Its stomach. Its heart.

I lifted the bird by its feet to shift its position, and the crisp slap of meat against wood whisked me back to my grandfather's butcher shop. The scene rose fresh before me, with its smack of screen door and smells of blood and sawdust, and my grandfather poised before the butcher block. I saw myself too as a little boy, barely five years old, peering into the display case. Inside lay neat yellow rows of chickens' feet.

"Look, look what I made, Grandpa," I said, holding up my Etch-a-Sketch.

"Very good," he said, without looking. "Now go back there and sit down. I'm almost finished."

"But what do you see?" I asked.

He glanced at my picture and said, "A face."

I thought I'd made a flower, and told him so. He waved away a fly and hoisted the side of beef onto his shoulder.

"Stare at anything long enough and you'll see a face."

My grandfather swung open the locker door and stepped inside, his white breath trailing behind. Every time that freezer door hissed shut I was sure he'd get locked inside. Every time I waited in terror, the fluorescent bulbs overhead buzzing my brain until the heavy door would reopen. This time he emerged with a shiny rack of lamb in arm, hand-picked for what would be our dinner. I watched him select a clean knife then mumble something to himself, his lips barely moving. Behind his head hung gleaming meat hooks, the wall so white it hurt my eyes.

Back in Iowa, I stared down at the half-skinned owl before me and wiped more sweat off my forehead. I could still recall that voice of my grandfather's, so deep and resigned to his job. Before cutting into each fresh side of meat, he always mumbled the same thing. Foreign, Hebrew words. It was a ritual, all his own. A prayer, I would later learn, for forgiveness.

I shooed away the gathering flies and gently rolled the owl over onto its stomach, then carefully unfurled the rest of the abdomen. Low on its spine I could see the cause of death, the backbone severed, and with it a major artery. I tried to imagine the impact—the sudden glare of headlights, the crush of rushing steel against bone, the bird's small scared heart unknowingly pumping out its life. Feeling flush and suddenly dizzy, I stumbled for the schoolhouse.

Just inside the door, I blacked out for a moment. As the room slowly came back into focus, I noted all the relics from my woodswalks surrounding me—not only the bottles of owl pellets, but all the sorted out piles of leaves and lichens and bleached bones. The shelves, stacked with old books and letters and photographs. The room smelled suddenly stale and earthen, moldy.

"A museum," I whispered. "I'm living in a museum."

I poured myself a cup of cool water and sat down on the rocking chair next to the phone. I had to fight off the desire to sleep.

"Chris? Yeah, it's me. I'm up near the wings, now what?"

"How's the smell?" he asked.

"Not bad."

"Feeling sick?"

"No, not at all," I lied.

"Good," he said. "Well, you're going to have to start cutting. You know that big tendon between the shoulder and the breast?"

"Yeah."

"Cut it," he said.

"Just cut it apart?"

"Yeah, then work the skin back beyond the shoulder till you get to the elbow, or whatever the hell that is, it gets kind of confusing."

"Okay, then what?"

"Find that second arm joint and cut blindly into it. It's mostly cartilage and tendon, but once you start cutting it'll make sense. You've got to go around in a circle, sort of like you did at the knees."

I was struggling to absorb all he was saying. Mostly the cutting part. I drained my glass of water.

"Then what," I asked.

"Then you're home free."

"What about the head?"

"Oh, it'll get a little sticky up there, but just keep doing what you've been doing. It'll come."

"Anything else?" I asked.

"Yeah, Nature Boy," he said laughing. "Save me the liver."

For the next two hours I did everything as Chris told me. The skinning grew more difficult and intricate, more grotesque. The owl's exposed cranium stared back at me over its shoulder, vulture-like. I'd gone from fearing to now regretting what I'd begun, cutting at the skin more erratically, rushing to wrench the last bit still clinging to beak. Then, it happened. As the pelt tore free, my exacto knife nicked the cavity. Stomach juices poured out, the smell rank. There was no way I'd dig any deeper toward the chest.

I pushed aside the soiled newspapers with my elbows and scraped away any remaining fat from the pelt's underside. Lacking salt, I shook Borax over the entire surface and quickly kneaded it in with my palms, then set the pelt aside to cure in the sun's rays. I breathed in deeply, but the air seemed thin and hard to swallow.

Off to my right lay the denuded bird, shrouded now by circling flies. A pair of wasps fed on the open wound in its stomach. I felt repulsed, but had to admit I was no less the scavenger. I stepped forward, waved them away, and before I could stop myself, had grabbed my rusted wire cutters, clipped the legs off at the knee, and crunched between two vertebrae at the base of the skull. I stared at what was left of the owl's carcass one last time, then, like a butcher, wrapped it in the stained newspaper.

19 November. Around midnight. Lying in bed. Just came in from stargazing with binoculars. The moon with all her deep craters … her scars …

Definition: Anatomy
> *1. A branch of morphology that deals with the structure of organisms.*
> *2. The art of separating the parts of an organism to ascertain their position, relations, structure, and function.*

Okay, if possible for livers and hearts, then why not for one's soul or emotions? Our mechanisms of fight or flight? And what about memory, could it be physiological? Say, some hidden chamber existing within, now and again pulsing forth? Waxing, waning … Or is your past like some organ you can amputate, or replace? There's got to be some tangible reason why you can't extract yourself from Sybil. Some kind of cure …

22 November. Remembering my first Thanksgiving in Italy at Lua and Alessandro's place in Verona. How we had to quarter and stuff the poor

*turkey into a pot because they only had a stovetop. How Aless couldn't
conceive of a holiday that wasn't church-based. He was so funny, trying
to help by putting on a Bing Crosby Christmas cassette. Lua nearly
peed her pants. We were laughing so hard we couldn't even explain it to
him ... Back then I didn't yet know about his HIV. Celebration such an
easy thing when you're ignorant. A glass of wine. A laugh ...*

*27 November. Out crunching in the snow under the pines tonight. The
ground glowing blue, the stars sparkling. Dippers to the north and
to the southeast Orion, that great hunter. First real snowfall of the
season. That first pure hush of white. Covering us all, like some sheet of
forgiveness ... if it were only so simple.*

Once the owl pelt fully dried, I strung it on fishing line to float
over the schoolhouse's threshold. The bird's feet I stood upright,
its paired talons curled round a cleft stone near my bedside.
The severed skull, meanwhile, still soaked in a bowl of bleach
in the bathroom, though I would display it too on a prominent
shelf. Preserved, and thus honored. Or at least that's what I told
myself.

I imagine to an outsider's eye, all these bones and shards
and skins might not have appeared as part of a museum, but
something more suspect. A morbid shrine, or worse yet, a
morgue. And frankly, I couldn't blame them. On the surface,
my motivations seemed as murky as ever—the lines between
prey and predator, passivity and aggression all confounded in
me by now—my "collection" of bones and skulls indefensible.
An outsider wouldn't know each one's personal significance

unless I told him. And yet isn't that true of any object? Isn't the most precious value of any heirloom its story? Paige's shiny eyeglasses. Grandpa's butcher block. Those broken televisions in my father's basement. The sacred photos of Sybil on my shelf. Somewhere down the line all such holdings outlive their context, turning into dollar items at some garage sale, or worse still, discarded, dust. Somewhere down the line someone doesn't tell their story. They get buried, even from memory.

I had nothing left of my brother's. Not a lock of hair, a photograph, barely even a story. Nothing.

Yet I did of Sybil. Far, far too much history to just let slip away.

Three days after I skinned the owl, a cat showed up from out of the schoolhouse woods. A brown tabby with the same exact coloration and markings, the same owlish eyes. For days it circled the schoolhouse. At first I was afraid it was an omen, the spirit of the skinned owl, hungry for retribution. Then I wondered if perhaps it was merely hungry. Temperatures by then were steadily below freezing, daily snowfalls dusting the ground. I set out a bowl of food, and within a week the cat moved in.

I kept her. Helping preserve her life seemed the least I could do, for accountability. Because in the end, I had to admit to some wrongdoing. To the conceit my deepest quandaries could be satisfied by merely stripping away some skin. As if one could ever possess the essence of something like an owl. Or glean a motive beneath the sudden deaths of rabbits or infants, the death of innocents. Of innocence.

When I buried what remained of the owl, I chose the spot carefully—at the end of a row of towering black pine uphill of the schoolhouse, where I'd seen other owls perch. And when I dug the hole, I dug it too deep for any other scavenger to disturb, down below the frost line. I lay the owl in its final nest and upon the shroud of newspaper sprinkled select objects: a shiny acorn, an oval-shaped creek stone, three thistles, and a shard of chert. To me, each found item possessed a special meaning and story. Stories I'd gathered from the surrounding woods by hand and hoped might keep the owl company, the way pharaohs once took trinkets into the tomb. I got up from my knees, filled in the hole, and tamped down the earth.

I didn't stop there, though. Couldn't, at least not yet. Over the grave I embedded four twigs, one in each corner bowing toward center, then laced them all together along with three of the owl's choicest tail feathers. As I stood there, they twisted in the breeze, like a tiny mobile suspended over a crib.

Deep inside, I knew the structure probably wouldn't last past winter, knew by then preservation itself was an unnatural act. Nonetheless, I marked the spot. Made it a place to which I could return. And if I'd only known the words, I would have mumbled my grandfather's prayer. Twice, to be safe.

A sharp breeze bit at my cheek and I looked around, suddenly concerned someone might be watching. My guilt, however, had less to do with the owl than with my own shame. I never buried anything in my life, did I? Never let go. I'd always thought that was because I cared too much, but now I wasn't so sure anymore. Maybe I cared too little. Maybe I wasn't too soft inside, but too callous?

I grabbed the shovel and headed for the schoolhouse. I was late for class in town.

History

There is a moment in the movie *Field of Dreams* when several figures first emerge from the edge of a cornfield—a handful of banned ballplayers from the notorious World Series of 1919. They step out like ghosts from between rows of shimmering stalks, still outfitted in their old uniforms and dated haircuts. At first their movements are slow and disoriented, their eyes squinting at the outfield's sudden expanse and light. As the soundtrack jokes, what they walk out onto isn't heaven—only Iowa. Over the course of the film, though, these fallen athletes do receive a shot at redemption on that rural ball field, a chance to replay and undo their past.

I can well imagine this cornfield scene projecting somewhere in the back of my head when I first drove out to Iowa. As if in slipping away from New York I could magically start my life over, fresh. Forgiven.

As if at the schoolhouse, I might wipe my slate clean.

5 December. Slight break in the weather today. A thaw. Morning woodswalk muddy between patches of snow. Hopping from one white island to the next, leaving footprints. Pawprints, too. Cat following me the whole way… kind of nice having her around…

Later. Drove over to Kalona's grocery this afternoon for bulk grains and sorghum. The Amish had turned out their cattle to graze on corn stubble, taking advantage of the melt. Their laundry out again, too. Drab dresses, dishtowels, corsets. Down the road, children's boots on the stoop outside their schoolhouse. Pulled over to watch dismissal. The kids walking the muddied roads beneath their wide-brimmed hats and bonnets, their books in arm. Stole a peek in the window. One-room like mine, yet crowded with desks. A squat brown woodstove in one corner and a whole wall of blackboards scrawled with arithmetic and bible verses, erasures.

When I got back to Redbird's schoolhouse I scanned its interior, wondering where its blackboards once hung. Tina had mentioned they'd done minor renovations to the eastern wall back in the mid-1960s, adding a side door, the fireplace, and chimney. Once again, I stood before its stone inscription—

Dolce Far Niente—thinking maybe I'd only scraped the surface thus far. Did a secret code to my renovation, my forgiveness, lay deeper still within the schoolhouse's walls and echoes?

The next week I started tracking down more on the schoolhouse's history than what Tina had told me. As it turned out, Iowa's main Historical Society was still located right in Iowa City (not in its capital Des Moines), a holdover from pre-statehood days. From a time before state lines pushed further west into the Indian Territories. While in town one afternoon for classes, I stopped in at the Society's library and archives.

I quickly learned Iowa's soil was rich in schoolhouse history, too. The Iowa Territory's first one-room schoolhouse dated back to a log cabin in 1830, built by eager residents of a settlement that only lasted three years. The abandoned building was subsequently squatted in, then cut up for firewood. By 1858, the new and growing State of Iowa passed legislation requiring each township to provide free elementary education, and one-room schoolhouses began sprouting up across the land. At the turn of the twentieth century, Iowa led the nation in rural schools, boasting nearly fourteen thousand! Now I just needed to find my schoolhouse.

With the help of a librarian I was led to a topographical map of Johnson County, dated 1900 and divided into its twenty townships. I ran my fingers over the map's grid west of Iowa City until I found a road that looked like Black Diamond. At the time, it was dubbed Old Man's Creek Road, and the road followed the creek and the creek branched to the north amid a cluster of ridges and trees, just like it did at Redbird Farm's edge today. That point on the map was nestled in the southwest corner of what was then called Union Township.

From there I went to the microfilms, scanning county superintendent records. It felt like I was in a detective novel, rummaging through dusty files and shelves for clues. One roll referenced "Teachers' Annual Reports." I asked the librarian.

"Oh, we've got the originals of those," she said. "Back over here."

We walked to the rear of the library where she climbed a stepladder toward a high shelf.

"How far back do you want?"

"I don't know," I said, "as far back as you've got."

One by one, she pulled down five cumbersome ledgers and lay them out on a wooden table. Each was tied with twine and bound in faded soft leather. A few of their corners had worn through, raw threads of cloth peeking out. Carefully I slid the most recent book toward me and undid the brown knot. Lifting its cover, I almost expected moths to float up into the air. What I found instead were yellowed pages, hundreds of them.

I flipped to the section marked Union Township, then back through the years until in 1956 I found a name I recognized—Jim Walters, the bluebird guy. The page listed him as eight years old then, and his sister Julie at age ten. Off to the right was their mother's signature: Paige Walters. Thirteen students were listed on the roster for that year, ranging from ages five to thirteen. The preceding page recorded their teacher's signature and the school's heading. My schoolhouse had a name after all: Union No. 9!

Near the bottom of the page was a space for suggestions concerning supplies. The teacher, perhaps not yet knowing 1956 would be Union No. 9's last year of classes, wrote:

- 4-6 new chairs to fit the height of our recitation table
- a hectograph
- some cement or gravel around door
- less mice!

I continued paging backwards, checking the Walters kids' attendance through previous years until their names disappeared into other names, the records sifting back through the Second World War, the Depression, WWI. With each successive ledger the schoolmarms' calligraphy grew more flowery, their names murmuring like music—Ila Wade and Dorothy Driscoll, Luella and Consolata, Daisy, Grace. Meanwhile, the pages themselves became more and more brittle, separating from bindings, fading, crumbling. In 1911, all the names gave out. I turned the page forward again.

January 8, 1912. Union No. 9 is born into history.

I closed my eyes and tried to imagine the day. January 8th— the dead of winter. Must have been below zero, even without wind-chill. Leaning into that wind comes Anna Rohret, the new teacher, arriving at the schoolhouse past dawn to start a fire and haul water from the creek for the children's washbasin. She sets down the bowl and the bucket, pauses, then reaches for the broom. Though she'd come and anxiously swept the floor last evening, she does so again—so many mice droppings. She sits and stokes the stove, quietly watching her breath in the air, trying to melt the snow from her skirt bottoms. She is thinking about her forenoon lessons. Thinking about what she'll do with her $42 pay come the end of the month.

At 8:50, she glimpses Maynard and Hazel Thomas trudging their way up the road, all bundled up and holding hands, their mittens a bright red against the snow. She jumps up and writes her name clearly on the blackboard. She steps back, then adds Miss, and the date. When the children finish kicking their boots against the stoop, she shows them in to the cloakroom and where to set their dinner pails. At five minutes past nine her other two students, the Halstead children, still haven't arrived. She glances out the window one last time and decides to begin. She clears her throat and says, "All right children, this is your new Jones Reader. Now turn to page—"

"Excuse me. Hello?" said the librarian.

"Huh?"

"It's closing time."

"Oh, sorry. I must've drifted off."

I returned the ledgers to their top shelves, then slowly drove home in darkness. By the time I rounded the last bend toward the schoolhouse, flurries were falling in the cast of headlights. Once inside, I hung my coat on a hook and turned up the thermostat. Too cold now for the fireplace alone. I pulled over a chair near the floor grating and warmed my toes. The floor joists creaked with the heat. The wind outside, pressing against the walls.

13 December. Feast day of Santa Lucia. Wish I were in Venice to light a candle. Should call Alessandro, but still too early in San Francisco. Tonight maybe…

Snowed again, third heavy day in a row. Drifts rising up and over the northern deck. Should I be worrying? Yesterday was the start of second shotgun season, and early this morning Tina showed up at my door with two neighbors, boys really. They shot a buck near dusk then lost its trail in the dark at the edge of Tina's property. We split up into pairs in the 60-Acre woods, and after an hour of thrashing through the Multiflora and snow my partner and I heard two shotgun blasts—a signal. Down near the gate we found the other boy waiting. The buck's severed head lay in his truck's bed. "Only thing worth salvaging," he said. "Coyotes."

Despite my resolution to leave questions of prey and predator behind, I couldn't stop thinking about the abandoned buck and later that day went back out to search the creek banks. Each of my exhales frosted before me, the surrounding floodplain frozen so hard my knees ached. After a quarter of a mile I noted a trail of red dots staining the snow. They reminded me of all the cardinals, who hadn't left for winter. According to Tina, that's how Redbird Farm got its name. Back on a cold and snowy January in 1964, she and Vance bought its first parcel and were walking the land noticing puffed red birds in the bare branches, decorating each tree like Christmas ornaments.

Tina also told me it wasn't unusual for a deer to circle back to its territory, even if shot there. "The pull of home," she called it. At the curve in the creek where the buck had crossed onto

Redbird, the water ran swift, its banks barely frozen. I tried to gauge the creek's width and icy depths against the sheer panic that must've propelled the injured buck across. By the time he returned, he might well have lacked the strength to re-cross and lay down momentarily to catch his breath. And on this bank he remained, a few feet shy of the water, beneath a leaning mulberry.

I stood beside that spot, beside what remained of the buck. Overnight the coyotes had eaten most of his hindquarters, a few splintered ribs poking through the torn muscle. One exposed femur showed signs of a smaller animal's gnawing and nearby lay bird prints among the strewn hair—the chain of scavengers well-defined and clearly urgent in winter. But one question remained: had the coyotes arrived before or after the buck expired?

I felt dizzy and sat back on a tree stump to catch my own breath. Overhead, clouds drifted and crows circled. The pull of home, I thought. Of New York. That strong, still.

15 December. Sunrise at 7:40 this morning, and no further south along the ridge than last week. Still between the ninth and tenth pine tree. Sometimes it's like time really can stand still out here… well, at least in my head. Meanwhile, the dusks are lengthening each day by the minute. The solstice nearly upon us. Less than a week till Sybil's birthday. What to do? What to do?

The prospects of talking, or rather *not* talking to Sybil for her birthday felt overwhelming. Instead, I focused on what was in front of me next—tapping into some oral history on the schoolhouse. Jim Walters seemed the most logical place for me to start, since he still lived only four or so miles away, now with his own family and farm. I drove over and found the front yard littered with his projects-in-progress: half-finished birdhouses, garden trays stockpiled with acorns and oak saplings, outcroppings of salvaged wood and discarded radials. A flagpole's halyard chimed in the wind beneath a Greenpeace flag, the family dog wagging its tail by the front door.

Inside, the house smelled sweet with yeast. Jim had been up working since 5 AM. His flannel shirt blanched with sifted flour. He baked sourdough for the food co-op in town, the best they offered.

"You sure you got time to talk?" I asked.

"Oh, yeah. Want some tea?"

"Sure."

I spread photocopies of the Annual Teachers' Reports on the dining room table, while Jim fetched two mugs. He poured hot water then leaned over the reports.

"Oh my, look at that. 1956, Mrs. Smalley. There's Karla and Grace, Emery. Yep, there I am. Huh, got a C in Geography."

"Deportment issues too," I pointed out.

"Yeah, well …"

He sat down and ran his freckled fingers over the old records.

"So what was the schoolhouse like back then?"

"Well, as you can see there were only five or six families worth of kids at most. Nothing like today's schools. No buses. No cafeterias. We'd walk to school and carry our own lunch pails."

"And the classes?"

"The teacher would work with one age group at a time, but of course we all picked up bits and pieces. I remember there was a lot of self-study time."

"The older kids help you?"

"Sometimes. Mostly they'd terrorize us. Oh you know, with stories. Snakes in the privy, teachers with warts ..." He paused for a sip of tea. When he lowered the mug, tiny crystals of honey glistened on his bushy red mustache. "I remember we had to get polio shots round about then. '55, '56. They told us the needles were so big they'd go in one side of our arm and come out the other."

"Anyone get polio?"

"No, and there weren't any snakes either. Least not in the outhouse."

"What about toilet paper?"

"Hmm, seems likely but I don't recall. Maybe we used hickory leaves, or the wish book."

"Huh?"

"The catalogue, from Sears," he said standing up. "Excuse me a sec."

He walked back through the kitchen and out the door. I could hear tins banging out on the porch where he kept his oven. When he re-entered a fresh loaf lay cradled in his mitt.

"Apple butter on this?"

"Yours?" I asked. "You bet."

He brought a Ball jar and knife to the table and broke off a piece of bread with his hand. Steam rose in the air, the aroma alone thick enough to swallow. We buttered our slices and ate in silence. On the mantel behind him spread photographs of his wife and son. A whole life, I thought. A wholesome one.

Jim scanned the reports, smiling. "Of course the best part of school was recess. Catching ground squirrels and going on the swings, sledding in winter. Oh, and helping tend the Yoder kids' horse. They came to school in a buggy. We'd each take turns feeding and watering her. She was a great old horse."

"The kids drove themselves?"

"You know those Amish, they do everything themselves. And do it right, too. Clean living. Clean farming. Forty to eighty acres tops, not like the rest of these chemical farmers. Did you know the DNR did a study a few years back and Old Man's Creek rated the highest concentrations of insecticide in the whole state? We tried to pass a bill that would restrict spraying locally, but not a single farmer would give even twenty feet of crop for their children's sake."

He was on his feet again, moving back toward the kitchen.

"If you told anyone ten years ago they'd be drinking bottled water today, they'd have laughed at you. Here, in America?! Nah, that's only in places like France or Italy."

I followed him out to the enclosed porch, where he started pulling out other loaves of perfectly golden bread from his oven.

"Internal clock," he said pointing to his head.

All around me were stacked sacks of flour and dusty seed trays. In the spring, Jim planted annuals for a local golf course, and in autumn harvested his own pumpkins and potatoes. Baking was his winter's work, and he did everything by hand from mixing and kneading to bagging and delivery.

"Yeah, those Amish, they've got it right. They're the ones you should be talking to. Still using one-room schools. Had to go all the way to the Supreme Court to resist consolidation. You know, that's this country's biggest problem, not family values or crime, but mobility. The average person moves every three years now, and not just across the street but across the country. So of course there's no sense of community or accountability. There's no damn commitment."

Jim's voice had started to rise, cracking almost. I averted my gaze, as his sermon could well have been for me. There I was, a thousand miles away from my home ground, and still running.

"Oh hell, now you've got me up on my soapbox," he said. "Here, why don't you help me bag some of those."

I set down my notepad and reached for a loaf. Its crust was still warm, its shape filling my palms. Something solid and simple you could count on, for sustenance. I slid the bread into the bag and set it on the table. Nearby, Jim bent over his formed dough, gently scoring, then sprinkling them with well water.

17 December. Last night, a sudden warm front must've swept through the bottoms, because the whole world looks married to ice this morning. The schoolhouse and hillside, frozen in a capsule of time...And tonite, 11 degrees without windchill. Out splitting more firewood beneath the moon. The logs shattering apart. Felt good to be breaking things. Still kind of pissed about Workshop this week. That classmate accusing me of being "absent" from my writings? I felt like yelling, "Wait a minute, isn't this supposed to be Fiction class?" Anyway, I'm in those characters. Every damn last broken one.

18 December. Met with Marcia Smalley today—Union #9's last teacher, 1954–56. Told me a few more tidbits, like how the kids would raise one finger to talk, two to go to the outhouse. How "every other Yoder child had curly hair." Her husband was home, too. He himself a student back in the 30s. Remembered Maynard Thomas, one of those first four students from 1912. Said his widow's still alive and living just down the road! Got to interview her ...

As it panned out, Maynard's widow wasn't much help. Sweet and spry for her ninety-three years, unfortunately her memories played out like tape loops that repeated every twenty minutes or so. And from what I could gather, her griefs outnumbered her gratitudes. Nowadays she was housebound and relied on neighbors to bring her groceries each Thursday. She served me juice and cookies and together we sifted through old photographs.

She kept picking up one of her husband, in which he stood beside their barn door. Kept tracing the outline of his hat and shoulders—the photograph's gloss long worn, one of its corners torn. Then she'd gaze out the window at the dusk, as if expecting him in from chores any moment.

That night, I stood before my bookshelf for several minutes before finally pulling out my thick envelope of photos. I could feel its mass in my palm, its pull. I tried to leave it at that, but failed. After opening its flap, I thumbed through the stack. Sybil in Coney Island and Corfu. In sunshine and swimsuits, sharp profile and soft focus. Caught in stride on cobblestone alleyways, city sidewalks, beachfronts. I brushed each and every one's surface with my fingertips. Each one's feeling of forever.

19 December. Schoolhouse door frozen shut this morning. Had to kick my way out, then dig the car out of a snowdrift ...

At the Johnson County Recorder's Office, I unearthed more clothbound ledgers from the past. Huge tomes so heavy they were stored on shelves made with built-in rollers to help you slide them in and out. Aptly labeled "transfer books," they listed past transfers of land titles. I located the pertinent volumes and began trying to reconstruct the puzzle of past grantors and grantees of what was now Redbird Farm. Beside me flitted young law clerks and real estate agents, eagerly flipping through the stacks to photocopy current deeds, then rushing out again. Meanwhile, I remained for hours on end, methodically turning pages and watching acreage shift hands and shapes back through history. My newest obsession taking hold.

One deed I uncovered, dated the 6th of July 1911, marked the very sale of land for the schoolhouse's construction—"8 x 10 rods conceded to the school board in consideration of the sum of $50." Other still older handwritten deeds were sealed in March of 1874 and January 1869. Transcribing the successive landholders' names confirmed how I'd heard the Old Man's Creek valley was settled—the Germans grabbing the rich bottomland first, the Irish arriving later and fanning out. Prior to 1860, all land transfer records disappeared. Courthouse fire, said the first entry.

Wedged into the corner of one shelf lay a squat leather journal, of which the Recorder's Office staff seemed only marginally aware. Its soft cover was vanilla brown and rimmed with remnants of gold stenciling, its surface smelling like barn dust. Inside lay a trove of beautifully hand-scripted field notes and sketched plats. Most of the surveyor's reference points were trees: ash and elm, birch, twin white oaks, a couple of posts in the prairie, wood culverts, a slough. I'd seen photographs of such men at the Historical Society; out in the field with their Vernier compasses and thick coats, tiny icicles in their beards.

I stood there in that recorder's office with its mauve carpeting and Venetian blinds, the steady hum of its Xerox machine behind me. All its sundry clerks were busy in their own little cubicles, typing or scribbling away, tearing off receipts, cross-referencing. All their actions so small and seemingly banal, yet here were the modern caretakers of history. People who stayed put, day in and day out. Balancing the books, taking account. Committed to something larger than themselves.

20 December. More snow during the night. Radio said only a couple inches, but surfaces can be deceiving. Drifts rising up to the windows now. Feels like I'm getting buried alive. On the opposite hillside, eleven horses up to their withers, all facing East …

Earlis Rohret was a neighbor who farmed a mile west of the schoolhouse. I'd heard he had a history book of his own—a thick family genealogy compiled by a distant cousin. He showed it to me one day when I came inquiring after Union No. 9's first teacher, Anna Rohret. Among the varied pages of his family branches, we found references to several Annas, only two of whom were distinct possibilities. One was married, which by 1912 wouldn't have necessarily excluded her. In the 1800's, schoolmarms were typically forbidden from marriage, or even dancing at socials. Women rarely ever taught school until the Civil War made it a necessity.

With noted pride, Earlis recounted how Rohrets were among the first to settle Old Man's Creek valley. His great-great-grandfather, Wolfgang Bauer Röhrert, was one of the few Bavarian soldiers under Napoleon to survive the Russian campaign of 1812. Departing Europe for good, he and his wife landed at Baltimore on Rosary Sunday in October 1840, and by November 11th trudged through three feet of snow up the fertile Old Man's Creek bottoms. As the family book tells it, Wolfgang asked his wife, "What do you think of the place?" to which she replied, "Well, there is wood and there is water, and where there is wood and water we can always get along."

Their sons went on to fell and split the timber that framed the first state capitol in Iowa City, most probably hauling it along the gravel road due north of the schoolhouse that still bears the Rohret name. Today, however, Earlis' only son worked with computers in another state, and though Earlis didn't admit it aloud, I could sense his being the last in a long line of farmers weighed heavily on his old shoulders. What would become of the land? Who would be its titleholders and caretakers?

In truth, however, who's to say the Rohrets had rights to their land to begin with? At the time Wolfgang Röhrert first staked his claim, the valley was still technically Tribal Land. In fact, I'd learned "Old Man's Creek" derived from the native name *"Push-i-to-nock see-po."* According to legend, nearby Sauk villages along the Iowa River would send old men, women, and children up creek to hide in times of imminent danger. George Catlin's maps of 1840 attribute most of the Iowa Territory to either the Sauk & Fox or Ouisconsin Indians, though varied tribes had made "Iowa" their home ground—the Potawatomi, the Ottawa, Sioux, Ioway, Winnebago. Of them, only the Mesquakie (Fox) had the prescience to pool resources and purchase land for a settlement that remains today near Tama, Iowa. All the rest were forced elsewhere by treaties serving westward expansion.

Like any given day in the woods, the natural flow of history is also in part about predation, about coyotes. The dispossessed, if not outright swallowed, eventually get written out. Plowed under. Buried. Yet the past, howsoever muffled, still strives to be heard.

There is a story I'd been told about my father. That for the first two and a half years of his life he never uttered a word. His family had already nicknamed him *de shtimmer* (Yiddish for "the mute"), when one day he suddenly spoke. A complete sentence, in fact—"Mr. Edelman, the iceman, is here," he said. Then, without any ceremony, he continued to converse like the rest of the world.

Decades later, by then married and a father, he began suffering from chronic depressions. He'd spend weeks, sometimes months silently sitting on our couch—to me, something of a cipher, a sphinx. As a family, we would similarly keep quiet about his illnesses, keeping them safely closeted within the house.

A few years after he died, I also overheard a story about his father—my grandfather—the one who worked in a hat factory. It seems he didn't die of a heart attack as I'd always been told, but one day went into that factory and hanged himself from the rafters. Whatever his reasons, he chose to choke back the words. Perhaps it had something to do with why he first ran away to America. Or perhaps with silences his father, or even his father's father, chose to carry. Of these, I can only wonder. All such secrets lay safely buried with them across the ocean.

Still, I don't doubt the natural flow and loss of history, both personal and collective, are equal parts denial as well. In truth, I didn't need look any further back than myself for evidence of such. What I couldn't bury, I simply tried to outdistance. To erase from sight. We are all of us, to some extent, descendants of ice.

21 December. Sybil's birthday. Somewhere in New York, perhaps at this very moment, she is walking down some sidewalk. Perhaps even on Lexington uptown, wearing a dark dress and heels, or, more likely, warm tights and boots. Her coat pulled close, her cheeks flush. I should call. I could, just pick up the phone and dial. Break this silence. This heartbreak. Nothing's stopping me. Just a simple call to say happy birthday and… and what? What could I possibly say now? I'm sorry? Goodbye? Hello? And anyway, why would I be calling—to make her feel better, or just myself?

Later. Had to get away today, so drove out to the Indian mounds near Amana for solstice, but couldn't seem to locate them among the snowdrifts. Eventually had to wander back to the car. Too damn cold.

Still later. Nighttime and candlelight now. The wax dripping beside this journal. The moon above finally falling west. This long day will pass. This longest of nights. This longing. No, I will not take out that envelope of photos. Not tonight.

Geology shows North America's last great glacial advance drifted only halfway down into what is now central Iowa, retreating completely by 10,000 B.C. Over the next several thousand years, the spare conifers that migrated down with the ice were gradually replaced by oaks, then prairie grasses. While no evidence of Paleo-Indians has surfaced near Redbird Farm, food-grinding implements dated over five thousand years old have been unearthed elsewhere in Iowa.

One afternoon, I found a more recent relic in my Redbird mailbox. Jim Walters' older sister sent me copy of a black and white photograph she'd taken within the schoolhouse in the early spring of 1956—during those last couple months of that final class of Union No. 9.

Back uphill and indoors, I held the square photograph at its edges and scanned its silvered surface. Spanning the upper frame was a segment of the alphabet, the letters J-U stenciled in upper and lower case, block and cursive. Beneath them hung a string of paper-doll snowmen and a small American flag. A snippet of assigned homework chalked on the blackboard's slate:

1. Tell how each of the following factors resulted in destruction of fur bearing animals:

a. People in Europe wanted furs

b. Early settlers cleared land

c. Early settlers needed food and clothing

Yet what drew my attention most stood in the foreground, the children all tightly bunched and posed. On the picture's flipside, penciled in a schoolchild's slanted scrawl, were the names of the Yoder children, Mrs. Smalley, and all the other students save for one little boy. Perhaps he was sick that day. Or maybe he was absent on purpose, not wanting his face to be recorded.

I spent a lot of time flipping the photograph over and back, matching faces with the names of classmates I felt I'd come to know. Children who until then were only names now stood before me, forever frozen in time: the light glancing off Mary's eyeglasses, Grace with a finger in her mouth, Helen crossing her thin arms. I counted three forced smiles, a pair of eyes looking askance, and several scuffed knees. Behind them all towered Mrs. Smalley, her lipstick dark and precise.

For days I studied their faces, trying to spot clues in their young cheekbones as to how their lives had taken shape and where they'd wound up. Something telltale in each gaze that might augur the choices that had become careers or divorces or children of their own. The kind of choices we all come to celebrate or regret.

Or in my case, avoid facing.

Around this time I also received unsettling news from Tina. After thirty years of stewardship, she was now planning to sell the schoolhouse and its land. All four hundred ninety-six acres. The work and costs of upkeep were growing too taxing for her. She'd begun negotiations with Iowa's Department of Natural Resources, so she could ensure preservation of the property in its natural state for at least another seventy-five years. She couldn't predict when the sale would eventually take place, but at least wanted me to know.

In retrospect, it doesn't surprise me that I chose not to document the events and facts of that particular day in my journal. Of either the specific light in Tina's house or the discomfited look on her face as she told me the news, or my frigid walk back uphill. En route, I took a detour to the site of the fallen buck under the mulberry tree. By now its spare remains had dried like hemp, its hide frozen stiff among bare ligaments and bone. Half-buried in the snow. Holding out still, if irredeemable.

I stood there and wept.

24 December. Christmas Eve. Alone. The schoolhouse windows coated with crystals. Like looking out from inside a freezer…And here I thought I'd found the perfect haven. What a joke. You can hardly tell whether you're hiding out from the past, or in it …

Homework

❧

15 January '93. In flight. Somewhere east of Chicago and leveling at 30,000 feet. Amazing, how quilted everything looks from this height. How ordered, and planned ...

Heading to Albany for my nephew's birthday party. Roller-skating this year. Should be good for some much needed giggles. Booked my return flight out of LaGuardia. Going to give myself an extra couple of days to research my own history in Brooklyn. Try to get past my past. Like the flight attendants say, "Your nearest exit may be behind you."

Twice a year, no matter where I was living, I tried to be present at my nephew and niece's respective birthday parties. We saw so little of each other it seemed an important day to share with them, especially since their parents had divorced. My sister still retained the old grey three-storied house in Albany, NY, and years back our mother had moved upstate to be closer to her growing grandchildren. Their houses weren't prior homes of mine nor anywhere near where I'd grown up, so my visits were just that, visits. No sentimental trips down memory lane, no trumpeted returns. In truth, I'd often feel displaced.

Nearing the East Coast, I could glimpse the growing tangle of roadways and old traffic patterns below, all those unavoidable tolls and potholes. While I knew my family all loved one another, communication wasn't our best suit and somehow we always wound up feeling, well, gridlocked.

A sculptor friend had recently lent me Gaston Bachelard's *The Poetics of Space* to further spur my thoughts on the schoolhouse and my woodswalks. In flight I'd cracked it open to the Table of Contents, which listed chapters exploring the structures of nests and shells and houses. Barely ten pages in I had to pause. "The house we were born in is an inhabited house," wrote Bachelard, "...and has engraved within us the hierarchy of the various functions of inhabiting. We are the diagram of the functions of inhabiting that particular house, and all (our) other houses are but variations on a fundamental theme."

I reread the paragraph several times. As the plane began its descent, I vowed to push beyond distancing myself on this trip, to instead try observing my family as closely as I'd learned to track things in the woods. Maybe their behavior could reveal something fundamental about who I'd become.

My nephew was turning ten that year. Michael was the first grandchild in our family, though my father had died just prior to his birth. No doubt his arrival brought some measure of grace to my mother's mourning, not unlike my birth must have in the wake of my lost brother. Watching her greet her grandson at the party, I recognized her all encompassing embrace. Loving, yes, but a touch needy, too.

My sister, meanwhile, was busy with preparations—laying out the tablecloth and paper plates for cake, counting candles. Since the divorce she'd grown understandably harried as a single parent. She'd also become more serious and guarded. During the breakup her ex-husband had turned vindictive, often emotionally abusing her or manipulating their children. What triggered such irrational behavior was probably rooted in his own childhood, as he'd been abandoned by his mother at the tender age of six. In retrospect, I wondered if my sister had unconsciously chosen her own "broken bird" to marry, not unlike our mother had. Not unlike how I seemed obliged to keep nursing my same old wounds. My sister was now trying to break old patterns, but clearly paying for it. Part of me wanted to ask her about this. About how she got over the past.

I walked over to the table. "Want some help?" I asked.

"Sure," she said and pointed to a little pile of plastic forks and spoons. "Set those out, will you? I got to run and get the cake."

Okay, so maybe now wasn't the best time to ask.

Once all the other children arrived, we got them fitted for roller skates, myself included. Having never skated before, I inched out onto the wooden rink and proceeded to fall often. Playing the clown was the role I'd often assumed within our family—perhaps to counterweight my father's periodic depressions, or perhaps to convince myself I was different from him. As far as my niece and nephew were concerned, I was more than happy to offer pratfalls. I stumbled round and round the rink, and our laughter echoed off the walls. Then we all ate pizza and blew out the candles, and Michael tore open his presents beneath the flash of cameras. He even gushed over my gift—a pair of binoculars and beginner's birding book. The party, a romping and soaring success.

Over the rest of the weekend, I took turns visiting my sister and mother's homes. We stayed up late, trying to catch up on our respective lives, trying to talk about something beyond mere surfaces. But this was hard for us, and in the end I was unable to get my sister alone to talk further about her divorce. I shared several photographs of Redbird Farm I'd brought along, showing them how its horizon changed with the seasons, and my growing collection of animal bones and pelts. Admittedly, this new life of mine must have seemed very strange to my family of furnished homes and domesticity. Yet my remove, no doubt, was familiar.

On Sunday evening, I mentioned the oral histories of the schoolhouse I'd been conducting, and soon my mother was sharing tidbits of her Brooklyn youth. She reminisced openly about Ebbets Field and Pee Wee Reese and waiting in line for Sinatra outside the Paramount. About her parents' butcher shop on Avenue O near West 6th. Of sidewalks and skate keys. Yet when I tried to unlock skeletons from my father's family history, she grew reticent. Impatient.

"What is this obsession you have with bones and digging up the dead?"

I didn't answer her, couldn't. All I could sense was this wasn't strictly about my father or his father, or only about the past. It was about me, and now.

My mother stared at me in silence.

"Let it lie," she finally said. "Let it lie."

But I just couldn't. Not anymore.

Come Monday, I boarded Amtrak for Manhattan. As the train snaked its way alongside the Hudson River, I thought about my father. I imagined he too must have struggled to separate himself from what ailed his father—the weight and legacy of a suicide even harder to bear. Perhaps that struggle, and not surrender, was at the heart of my father's bouts with depression. And perhaps his father, in crossing the ocean from Europe, was desperately trying to leave something behind him, too. Something, ultimately, unshakeable.

Outside the window, Yonkers was passing and with the first glint of skyscrapers I thought of Sybil. I'd debated contacting her while in Albany, and half reached for the phone once. Part of me felt like it was the most natural thing in the world to do, while the other part fought to resist old impulses. Now, with only miles between us, even the remote possibility of bumping into her felt imminent. Unavoidable.

No way, I reasoned. *It's a city of millions. Relax. You can do this.*

Yet as the train barreled on through the Bronx, I gripped at the seat's armrest, feeling her presence growing nearer. Her voice. Her pull. My chest started buckling, short of breath. Soon the train was shunting past her very block in Spanish Harlem. I stared wide-eyed out the window, both yearning to catch a glimpse of her and fearful I would. And then the elevated tracks plunged below ground, into darkness and echoes.

Jesus, I thought, *a little melodramatic here, aren't we? Come on. Snap out of it.*

But I couldn't. I was staying at my old apartment on Lexington Avenue, to which I still held a lease and had sublet to a friend. Inside, everything remained more or less the same as I'd left it—the black couch and coffee table, the set of cheap dishes, the double bed. What felt more prevalent, however, was what wasn't present. Everywhere I looked conjured images of Sybil. Her makeup on the bathroom sink's ledge. Her dress peeking out of the closet. Her curved body among the morning's white sheets and *Sunday Times*. Her untied shoes beside the door.

I could hardly breathe and retreated to the city streets, but even there kept tripping over minefields of memory: the corner Korean grocer where I bought her flowers each Friday, the 8th Street Playhouse and Lincoln Plaza Cinemas, the Beekman. Every movie house and theater marquee screamed Sybil as its leading lady. Every museum and restaurant and subway platform we'd shared, all leapt out from the cityscape. I found myself haunting each one, half in terror of finding her, half in hope.

Eventually I wound up in Central Park, seated beneath a trellis of barren branches behind the band shell. In springtime, we'd come and stroll there beneath the fragrant wisteria. I sat there, trying to recall their blossoms' hue and smell, the precise feel of her hand in mine.

"This is crazy," I said aloud. "Get up. Get up off this bench, go do your research, and get the hell back to Iowa."

Among the dark recesses of the 42nd Street Central Library huddles room 84—The Jewish Division—down in the basement, as if half in hiding. Conserved within lie amazing documents, like breadcrumbs of a diaspora, wandering across borders and back through the centuries. My search, however, entailed something relatively recent and nearby, just downtown—that rumor about my father's father I'd been trying to confirm for years. I approached the front desk where a short woman stood sorting through piles of books.

"Excuse me, I'm looking for—"

She held up one hand as if stopping traffic, then pointed to the sign-in book at the desk's corner. I walked over, printed my name then hesitated before entering Iowa for my HOME ADDRESS. In the space marked REASON FOR VISIT, I simply wrote Personal. I returned to the librarian and waited for her to look up.

"So," she said. "You're standing there, so say something."

"I'm looking for old newspapers from the Lower East Side."

"Do you read Yiddish?"

"No," I admitted.

The old woman nodded and stared at me.

"Is that a problem?"

"For me, no. For you?" she shrugged. "You're the one who asked for newspapers."

She picked up a pencil and rolled it between her palms.

"Well, do you have any here?" I asked.

"Maybe yes, maybe no. Maybe you want to give me a clue?"

Now it was my turn to stare.

"A date, sonny. I need a date."

"Oh, I'm sorry. 1938. January 29th, 1938."

I'd already consulted a book on calendars to find out which date corresponded to the lunar month and Hebrew characters etched into my grandfather's tombstone. Like everything else surrounding the man, this too was partially obscured.

After a few minutes, the old woman returned with three boxes of microfilm. Before handing them over, she slowly and patiently explained about the different Yiddish presses: one, predominantly religious, another with socialist leanings, and the third's agenda lying somewhere between. Heading toward the viewing machines at the rear of the room, I passed several other researchers. Most were elderly and mole-like, hunched over desks with their noses deep in texts whose typefaces weren't only Hebrew, but German and French, Russian, Ladino.

As I scrolled through the microfilm I didn't feel like a detective this time so much as a foreigner, comprehending nothing but the pictures—one photograph of a smiling Franklin and Eleanor Roosevelt, another of Stalin clasping his hands, a caricature of Hitler with one eye obscured by exaggerated bangs. A few advertisements were in English, one for a vaudeville theater, another for Diamond Brand cream cheese. A dermatologist on Pitkin Avenue. Butterfingers for a nickel.

It wasn't until I scanned the most religious journal's microfilm and couldn't locate the 29th of January that I realized the date was a Saturday. That my grandfather, a religious, Orthodox man had not only risked a Jewish burial by committing suicide, but had literally hanged himself on the Sabbath. This fact, more than anything else I'd yet learned, pointed to the depth of his desperation and, for perhaps the first time, made this man feel real to me. Human, and vulnerable. Maybe even forgiven. It also revealed the roots of my family's deep denial—not only was my grandfather's final act inherently scandalous, but also bespoke of a helpless fracture of faith. Of course there would be no obituary in these Yiddish newspapers, no public mention of an act his own family wouldn't even share among themselves.

Just in case, I went upstairs to check the old *New York Times* indices. On that date in 1938, the *Times* cost only two cents and one of its leading headlines reported on a US representative who'd been slapped by a Japanese soldier at Nan King. Alongside ran another feature concerning FDR's national defense speech—the president calling for Navy buildups in the Great Defense Program. On another page I noticed a tiny article about a women's medical college in Romania, where Jewish students had been beaten with rubber clubs. An adjacent column read "League to Examine Jewish Petitions."

It felt very strange reading such headlines in retrospect, like having to watch the world on the cusp of spilling over into war and horror with your hands tied. As for the local obits in the *Times* that day? Only a ship owner and an oilman, two stage actors, and an ex-mayor of London. If the world at-large couldn't recognize the oncoming slaughter of millions of soldiers and civilians, how could I expect anyone to take notice of one small hat manufacturer on the Lower East Side? His death was destined to remain as silent and private as his act.

Yet here I write and speak his name: Avram Chaim Nissenbaum.

Outside the library, I sat on the stone steps facing Fifth Avenue trying to figure out what came next. I watched the tides of pedestrians ebbing and flooding with the changing traffic lights.

The tiny puffs of their breath disappearing in the cold air. I walked to the corner and bought a hot knish from a Pakistani street vendor. An immigrant like my grandfather, I thought, like so many in Manhattan's unfurling sea of faces. I turned up my collar and joined their flow, heading for a downtown train.

Snow flurries had begun by the time I climbed out of the subway at the edge of the Lower East Side, the edge of my history. Once, nearly all of my father's family lived cramped among these few square blocks. Now, not a one remained. Some, like myself, had scattered far away. The rest were dead. I wondered about the weather on that January day in 1938. Was there snow then, too?

I walked down Essex Street past the kosher pickle man ladling out sours and dills from deep plastic barrels. At one time my paternal grandparents owned two buildings nearby, numbers 5 and 7 Hester Street. They'd been purchased with a down payment my grandmother smuggled out of Eastern Europe sewn into the hem of her skirt. Money she'd earned running contraband to soldiers at the front, and ultimately paid for with her vision after sustaining a head-blow from the butt of a Cossack's rifle. At the time, my grandfather was already here in Manhattan, having emigrated before WWI broke out, leaving her and their first child behind. The plan was to send for them soon, but eight years elapsed before they were reunited.

As I searched Hester Street for those addresses, I too felt separated by the vagaries of history. Where my grandparents' buildings once stood now rose a housing co-op, a large complex engulfing the entire block where they later lived when my father was fourteen years old, in that fateful year of 1938. Damn it, I thought, yet another dead end.

Across the street, an old Chinese woman was sweeping fresh snow from a path behind her building. Beside her lay a tiny garden plot, fallow save for a few stubborn strands of green onion. In addition to my father, Avram Chaim had two other children, girls. The younger of those daughters had been the one to find him hanging in the factory. All three siblings, however, bore his suicide in silence. All three went on to bear their own children, and all three lost their first born sons—one at seven to an asthma attack, one at seventeen to a bolt of lightning, and one at seven months, my brother, to his malformed heart. These coincidences, of course, bore forth further superstitions and silences.

I trudged on to Elizabeth Street, now in search of the old hat factory. My mother only recalled the building number being low, less than one hundred. My father never spoke much, let alone about his father. None of his siblings remained for me to ask, and even if they did, it's hard to say what they might have revealed, or if I would have had the courage to ask. By all rights, I should have been carrying the Nissenbaum surname, the sole surviving son of the sole surviving son, but my father had it legally changed after facing repeated job discrimination in the 1940s. To a certain extent, I imagine the shedding of that legacy wasn't entirely wrenching for him. Perhaps, it came as a relief.

Once on Elizabeth Street, I glanced at each shop and entranceway. Chinese signs fronted all the old garment and fabric houses, all the new food marts and video stores. Chinatown was ever expanding, ever encroaching on the Jewish "*shtetls*" and Little Italy. Within second floor windows, however, hung the same sharp fluorescent light and hovering steam, only now Asian women and children were the ones seated behind sewing machines and sorting tables.

I walked up and down the block several times, peering at each address as if one might speak to me. I stared at each stoop, wondering if it was the one my grandfather had paused at before turning his key for the last time.

Halfway down the block, I noticed several policemen clustered outside their station house. While I'd already passed by, something suddenly occurred to me. I rushed over to the precinct's steps and pulled back its heavy door. Two officers brushed past, laughing. Another sat behind a tall receiving desk.

"This may sound a little strange," I started, "but uh, I'm wondering if you could help me?"

The sergeant swiveled in his chair and rested both elbows on the high desktop. Mostly, he looked bored.

"Well, my grandfather hung himself on this block and I, ... I guess I'm trying to find out where."

The sergeant's expression changed. "Here on Elizabeth Street, you say?"

"Yes."

He reached for a pad. "Okay, what's the address?"

"Oh, no," I said, "this was a long, long time ago. I'm just doing some...family research. I was hoping there might be records here, a report or something."

The sergeant leaned back in his chair, one of his cheeks puffing out with his tongue.

"This isn't some kind of joke, is it?"

I glanced at his badge and nameplate, then back at his eyes. "No," I said. "Do I look like I'm kidding?"

"Yeah well, you'd be surprised what comes through that door," he said. "Wait here a minute."

He walked to the other side of the room where he paused to whisper to a fellow officer then disappeared down a stairwell. After a few minutes he returned with yet another officer, much older and with reading glasses balanced on the tip of his nose. The sergeant pointed at me and the other man came forward, shook my hand, and introduced himself. He was from Records.

"Now, do you have any idea when this hanging took place?"

"Oh yeah. The end of January, 1938."

"1938," he mused, then made a quick sucking noise between his teeth. "If you'd showed up a couple months ago, I coulda maybe helped you out. We had to shred all them years. Purged 'em, lock stock and barrel."

I stared into his eyes, still waiting. Finally I said, "Statute of limitations?"

"It's got nothing to do with the law. We just don't have the space. Sorry."

He waited till I turned away first, then headed back across the room. I stood on, listening to his footsteps echo down the stairwell. The sergeant was back at his desk post. He brought two fingers to his forehead and saluted me. I stepped outside.

By then the snow was sticking—the street and the sidewalks, every fire escape, awning, and stoop freshly coated with flakes of white. The whole city's swirl of sound suddenly reduced to whispers.

I zipped my jacket against the cold. Purged, I thought, how appropriate a word, for even the documented past was destined to a kind of silence too, wasn't it? Everything, eventually forgiven to dust? As it turns out, that's what my mother had been asked to do by my father's family regarding the suicide—not necessarily to lie, but to let it lie. I guess they felt if something was left behind, then it didn't need be confronted. Clearly yet another lesson in retreat I'd imbibed, yet now needed to resist.

The next day I rented a car and drove out to Long Island. Like many families who slowly filtered out of Brooklyn following WWII, my parents too bought a house in the suburbs. That was in the spring of 1961, when I was a mere toddler. I took my first steps on that house's sunken living-room floor, spent my childhood running through its rooms, and slept under its roof for nearly twenty years. The roadways leading to that home were as familiar as the constellation of freckles on my skin, and for better or worse what lay within its walls had similarly imprinted me. Logically, I figured I should revisit this old address, too.

As I neared my childhood town I rolled down the car window, and the scent of the Great South Bay slowly returned to me. All my old haunts glided by one by one: my high school parking lot and the bowling alley, the Carvel shop—places where I should have first fallen in love as a teenager, but never did. Soon I was approaching my neighborhood, turning onto streets I'd bicycled daily on my newspaper route. I could recall each front stoop, each customer's face and varied tips. From time to time I still dreamt about that delivery route, about losing track of who owed what. About other tasks I'd left undone, other people I'd left in the lurch.

As I veered onto my very block, the house in which I'd grown lay just beyond the next bend. I eased up on the accelerator and coasted round the curve. Then, I blinked. Had I not known the adjacent homes, I might easily have driven right by. Our old house had been remodeled beyond recognition, its face now encased in stone, my bedroom window entirely erased. The yard too seemed foreign—the junipers and Japanese maple torn up by the roots. The beloved mimosa. In their stead, spread a layered rock garden.

"My God," I whispered, "it looks like a diner."

I didn't go knock on its front door. I didn't even get out of the car. I pulled away from the curb and didn't look back, my head in a cloud.

Miles away I regained my bearings, and headed toward the Brooklyn apartment where I'd spent the first year of my life. En route, I drove past the actual hospital where I was born. Our brick apartment building wasn't too hard to find, thankfully still standing, if indistinctly from all the others along Ocean Avenue. A vacant parking spot, right out front.

I approached its front vestibule and read the names listed beside each buzzer, not exactly sure what I was expecting to find. I'd neglected to ask my mother which apartment number had been ours, and even if I did, what could I possibly find inside there now. For years I'd tried to remember its rooms. To re-enter its kitchen, say, or its hallway. Or that small bedroom at the rear where I'd inhaled some of my first breaths, and where my brother had exhaled his last.

I'd always pictured its walls a pale blue. Venetian blinds across the windows and cobwebs in one corner. That forever smell of talcum and dusk. In reality, of course, I held no conscious memories of that space, held nothing but my own imagination. Returning to this old apartment's threshold now seemed about as ridiculous as would re-visiting my birth hospital's maternity ward. What could any of those little faces behind the glass possibly tell me now?

You *can't* go home again. Of course. Can't confront what's already passed. But then you can't entirely escape it either.

I got back in the car and for a while simply stared at the pigeons and seagulls banking overhead. Then, I started driving. At first anywhere just to be moving, but before I knew it found myself nearing Coney Island. Drawn there, as if by magnets. For years,

Sybil and I would come out by subway on summer weekends to indulge in all its deep fried clamor—the hot city sun beating down on us, half of Brooklyn lining the boardwalk, our beach towel littered with cool tins of *frutta di mare* and thick french fries, the stretch of our swimsuits against tanning skin.

Everything I thought I ever wanted was right there within arm's reach. And if not, within ten minutes a string of barking teenagers would hustle by dripping plastic bagfuls of "Ice Cream, Budweiser, *Cerveza Fria!*" One guy wore a huge sombrero, trudging up and down the beach taking Polaroid portraits. "Technicolor Happiness," he'd cry, "Technicolor Happiness!" And it was true, that was precisely how I'd felt. How we'd felt.

In certain ways our relationship was very much like an instamatic photograph, our eternal slice of summer. For me, as burning and blinding as the sun. Sybil was the first woman who'd ever taken any real interest in me, who sensed something beyond my reserve even worth approaching. So no wonder I fell into her waiting arms and spell. And for her, I suspect our tantalizing tryst soon turned into a safe, if distant, harbor. Here was someone she wouldn't need involve in her already complicated domestic life. Someone young and intense, yet clearly harmless and adoring.

Looking back, I also suspect that beneath our respective fantasies simmered some submerged hope, or fear against fear more likely, that one might actually rely on another's love. I don't think either of us could have imagined our firewords lasting a decade, if indeed either one was looking ahead. So who could blame Sybil or me for merely wanting to be loved? For wanting to keep basking in that summer's warmth and glow?

But now it was winter, a sharp wind chafing Coney Island's boardwalk. As I walked its planks, I could hear my footsteps among each gust whistling through the pilings. All else hung painfully quiet. The amusement rides all closed for the season, every sideshow and carny boarded up, the old Thunderbolt and Parachute Jump listing in rust and ruins. Not a single soul in sight.

I descended a staircase and headed out onto the snow-swept beach. It felt like I was in some foreign film, one more surreal than sad. Absurd. Down near the shoreline, chunks of broken ice gathered at the water's ebb, and overhead ran the long empty pier from which scores of fishermen would toss their hooks and traps come summer. Sybil always used to laugh about how they'd waste two pounds of chicken to catch a pound and a half of crab. Out on the water, a distant container ship labored against the grey sea. I watched its white hull slowly disappear among the far waves.

I turned back toward the boardwalk, beyond which rose the great curve of the Wonder Wheel. Once upon a time Sybil and I took a ride together. I could recall that night as if it were yesterday, gleefully handing the man our tickets and climbing aboard one gondola; the rainbow of neon lights glowing as we were lifted; the air thinning out over the midway. As we reached the apex, however, the Ferris wheel's great gears came grinding to a halt. All sound stopped, save for the hum of stars overhead and some child's squeal of terror below. I remember us hanging there for several minutes, each swaying with our relative qualms but saying nothing, silently waiting for the ride to start up again. For our teetering fate to play itself out. I could see the silhouette of those same rusted carriages, dangling still.

That old queasiness was rising inside me again, same as it had on our New Year's Eve helicopter ride. That same old holding pattern of suppressed doubts and vertigo. But now I knew what frightened me didn't revolve around heights or falling, or even death. It was the specter of *loss itself* that took my breath away. And no wonder, such shadows had run rampant in the house I was born into—crib death and a swinging noose quietly tucked within the very sheets of my swaddling, catatonic depressions among the couch cushions. A home whose prior casualties had unfortunately left all of us crippled and quivering at what the future might bring. So no wonder I could never look ahead, or would only chance getting so close to anyone. No wonder I couldn't face losing Sybil. No wonder I was living alone on a hilltop a thousand miles away.

21 January. Once again, in flight. Feeling tired, dead tired. Emotionally spent. All this running from the past and fearing the future. This fight or flight.

Down below, the skyscrapers are receding. They don't look all too different from trees in the woods, each spire struggling for airspace, for light...And here you thought all that would change in Iowa... Okay, time to take a deep breath and start anew. Again.

Social Studies

❧

On the 25th of June 1876, an unknown vocal teacher of the deaf tentatively presented a demonstration at the nation's Centennial Exposition in Philadelphia. Young Alexander Graham Bell's invention, while still in its early stages, nonetheless impressed a handful of esteemed scientists. Word spread about a device that would herald the dawn of a new age in communication, a device far more immediate and intimate than Morse code. Decades later, on the occasion of Bell's death, even rival inventor Thomas Edison would say, "(this) world-famed invention annihilated time and space, and brought the human family in closer touch."

Or so the story goes.

Of course there were others who held differing opinions. Mark Twain, for example, who less than fifteen years after the telephone's arrival wrote:

"It is my heart-warm and world-embracing Christmas hope and aspiration that all of us—the high, the low, the rich, the poor, the admired, the despised, the loved, the hated, the civilized, the savage—may eventually be gathered together in a heaven of everlasting rest and peace and bliss—except the inventor of the telephone."

Who knows what Twain would have to say today, in our satellite bouncing world of infinite access. When I returned from New York to my hilltop aerie in Iowa, however, cell phones still weren't yet the rage. I still hoped to disconnect at the schoolhouse, if not necessarily hide out. Yet one afternoon I came back from a woodswalk to find a plain cardboard box sitting squarely on the schoolhouse's stone table. A small puddle of melted snow spread on the floor with boot tracks leading back out the mudroom door. Taped to the side of the box was a message, penned in thick red magic marker—"Use This Or Lose Us"—beneath which was scrawled my friend Chris' signature, plus the names of a handful of other friends in Iowa City. I opened the box flaps to reveal a telephone answering machine.

At first I laughed, as I'm sure was intended. This wasn't the first time friends had voiced frustration with my relative seclusion. Tina had told me that while I was out of town one had literally driven out to the schoolhouse to make sure I hadn't frozen to death in the woods. Friends like that one shouldn't risk losing. I hooked up the machine and re-recorded my outgoing message five times until no hint of resentment could be discerned.

And initially, I liked the machine's convenience. I no longer had to unplug the phone each morning when I wrote, nor necessarily answer incoming calls if I didn't feel like it. Within the week, though, it felt like callers' voices were invading my space at will, echoing off the walls, demanding immediate replies. Nagging beeps and messages accrued, worst of all the calls that would come late at night then hang up. Those late night calls I myself was still tempted to make to New York. Part of me kept holding onto the belief that as long as I didn't talk with Sybil, we could avoid the finality of our separation.

Of course long before ever setting eyes on the schoolhouse I'd been avoiding all kinds of contact and noises in my life. I owned no television, no whirring microwaves or Cuisinarts, no vacuum cleaners or digital alarm clocks or even a wristwatch. Embarrassingly I read no newspapers or magazines either, preferring the world of fiction—living in books or in my head. As a consequence I knew little of national trends or world events and was a good ten years out of the loop on popular culture. In short, I'd be an extremely poor dinner guest, that is, if anyone would dare invite me. One old friend accused me of living in a perpetual state of hibernation. Another, of social dyslexia. Others just stopped telephoning.

First of February. Dropped to 10 below last night. The snow, thick-skinned. Andre's hauling in a flatbed of fresh hay, his horses filing down from the pasture. Got to get in gear myself. Empty the compost, see if the car will start. Got classes today, too. New semester and professors. McPherson's approach wholly different from Conroy's. In seminars he riffs like he's playing sax, his bebop and range mesmerizing. In workshop, he's more shy and quiet, raising questions rather than holding forth. Talking about the word and the world. Asking our storytelling to risk more civic engagement. To balance our retreats and our actions. Bridging word AND deed. Neighboring, he calls it …

Talking of neighbors, Tina turned up at my door this morning looking rattled and half-frozen. One of her dogs got disoriented in the snow, lost. I poured her a tea and by the time it steeped, the dog came scratching at the door. The relief on her face, palpable. She lingered on, talking about the weather—how this cold snap following January's brief thaw was fairly typical in Iowa. Of course what I wanted to hear about was news on the sale of the land, but didn't dare ask …

February. Winter. In New York City, snow would fall every year yet was never long-lived, and more briefly white. In Venice flurries occurred maybe once in a decade, and I never saw one during my three winters there. Yet on clear mornings, I could glimpse the tiny white peaks of the Dolomites off to the north. Distant, safe. But in Iowa, winter was up-close, personal, and not something you could avoid.

Each day I was greeted by its beauty, fresh domes of white balancing on the deck rails, thickening icicles reflecting rainbows off its southern eaves. And the closer I looked at the snow itself, the more intriguing its structure became; one minute floating down soft as cotton, the next jutting up from the ground like serrated knives; falling thick as quilts or in the faintest wisps windblown off the roof. I'd stand before the schoolhouse's big picture windows as if I were some lord overseeing his coffers, my crystal kingdom growing deeper and more muffled by the day.

"But aren't you getting cabin fever?" asked a friend on the phone one evening.

He'd called to jokingly ask if I needed instructions on how to operate my phone machine. Seems I wasn't returning calls quick enough.

"Cabin fever?" I said.

"Yeah. God, I'd go crazy out there all alone."

In my fireplace a log hissed. I knelt at the hearth and poked at the burning hickory, shifting the flames. I didn't think I was crazy being out here. I liked the distances and silences.

Or so I thought.

4 February. Been thinking about all the famous parties Tina and Vance used to host out here. All those big name authors who'd pass through town—Cheever and Vonnegut, Berryman, Carver—all walking about this same hillside. Maybe I should be sharing the wealth more, too? Writers are such social misfits, though. Creating characters on the page to play out what we can't muster face-to-face. Or maybe I'm projecting here ...

The next morning I headed out for my typical woodswalk. The early sun stippled my path and the snow crunched underfoot, the pine needles splaying overhead. I passed an old fence post with its twisted barbs to my left. To the right, a newly fallen elm. No, this wasn't crazy at all, I thought. I loved being out here in a world stripped down to such basics, each solitary moment rising before you to be met. I stood very still and held my breath, and in the distance could hear the lowing of a neighbor's cow.

When I took my next step, however, something burst from the undergrowth beside me. Ears down, tail raised, the rabbit rifled across the trail, a dark flash or two against the snow, then only the sound of its scampering in the brush. Then again, a thick silence descended. I knelt to witness the urgent marks the rabbit left behind—the length of each bound, the depth of the prints, the scattering of snow in their wake.

Obviously the rabbit must have heard me coming, yet had waited till the last possible second to run. Small animals' lives were probably often like this—their every step, every breath, a hairline of risk and survival—counting more on camouflage than confrontation, on cowering until they couldn't cower anymore. And with the sudden gust of a cold front, it struck me: I was one of their frail numbers, too.

Returning to the schoolhouse, I noticed a flashing red light on my answering machine and forced myself to press the red button. The message was from my mother, her voice reserved yet tinged with enough tremolo to make me call back right away.

"Anything wrong?" I asked her.

"Oh nothing, not really," she said.

Okay here we go, I thought, the cat and mouse of conversation in our family. Her tone sounded more weary than alarmed, so I figured whatever she called for wasn't too serious. She exchanged her usual updates and regards, then perhaps sensing I was close to hanging up, admitted to having just come home from visiting a cancer-riddled friend at the hospital.

"The doctors are only giving her two months," said my mother.

Giving, I thought, what a strange choice of words doctors use.

"That must be really hard," I said, trying to sound sensitive. "For you too, I mean."

My mother made a sound on the other end of the line, something between a sniffle and an exhale. Peevish.

"Look," she said, "I didn't mean to disturb you, but it's...I don't know, everyone around me seems to be dying."

"That's not true," I quickly replied, but then realized it was. Two old friends of hers recently. A brother-in-law. And now her old dog, which used to be mine, was incontinent and declining fast.

"It is true," she said. "It is!"

Outside the window I could see horses in the distance, pawing at the snow-covered pasture. I didn't know what to say. I thought about all the people she'd buried. Her parents. Her husband. A child. Thought about how she was slowly becoming the last of her family's generation. *Talk about loss. She's afraid. Show a little more compassion, for Christ's sake.*

"You know what she said this morning?"

"Who," I said.

"My friend! Aren't you listening?!"

"Yes, yes I'm listening. What'd she say?"

"She said she only had one more wish, not to die in winter. 'The ground's too cold, let me last till spring.' Those were her very words. Can you imagine?"

Again I searched for a response. I knew there was one that could make her feel better, but the words just wouldn't come.

"Oh damn it," yelled my mother, and I could hear the receiver fall against the counter in her kitchen. There were scampering sounds in the background, then her voice again, half sobbing. "The poor dog pissed the floor again. I'm sorry, can I call you back?"

" ... Sure," I said. "Of course."

---

6 February. Thermometer reads -12° and holding steady. -40° windchill! Watching juncos feed off the seed I spread out on the deck. And last night, saw a mouse inside, stealing food from Cat's bowl. Oh, almost forgot—horse-drawn sleigh ride with Andre through the 60-Acre woods yesterday! He had the team all rigged up with bells and blankets. The clicking hooves, the falling snow—felt like we were in some Russian novel. Invited him in for warm cider afterwards. Besides Tina, he's the first to cross my threshold since Thanksgiving.

8 February. Sewed up the holes in the tips of my gloves with a spare piece of string. Worked fine. Noticed my boot prints on the trail today, and how my left footstep tends to toe out. Strange, didn't know that until now. So much is ignorance. Or denial. Starting to wonder if this whole fiction writer persona is just another distancing device? Another excuse? Another holding pattern?

Recent quotes from readings:
   The character of an artist is revealed by the nature of his refusals.   *—Valéry*
   The slope of your roof is determined by the weight of snow.
         —Emerson

Notes from a diner in town last week: Carhartts hang near the door. George Strait on the radio. Slices of pie in the dessert case, thick crusts bulging with apple and peach, raisins. And that curvy waitress, carrying de-caf. Her apron perfectly perched on one hip. Need anything else, she asked … Those winsome eyes … No thanks, just the ticket.

Valentine's Day was coming and to avoid being alone I decided to throw a party for all the friends I knew from town. Schoolhouse Pond's ice was over a foot thick by then, and on the morning of the fourteenth I shoveled its surface, clearing away a skating rink in the shape of a huge heart. I then sprinkled its circumference with cherry Kool-Aid, though it quickly turned more brownish than red.

The day's weather couldn't have been better, windless with temperatures climbing into the mid 20s. The sun broke through too, the hillside literally sparkling as handfuls of guests arrived bearing skates and sleds and potluck desserts. Soon young children's laughter rang out. A real winter wonderland.

Meanwhile, I kept myself busy—refilling mugs of hot cocoa, tending the bonfire near the ice rink, playing the happy host. One of the guests was a dancer named Beth, whose choreography I'd admired at a recent university concert. At its end we spoke briefly, and I learned she too was a transplant from New York. Before I knew it, I'd invited her to the Valentine's gathering. She came with an old friend and fixings to make *glögg*, a popular winter drink in Sweden, where she once lived. I showed her where the pots were in the schoolhouse, then dashed out with more marshmallows for pond-side.

When next I came back indoors for supplies, she was still standing at the stove, stirring the dark liquid.

"Looks like sangria," I said, glancing over her shoulder.

"Yeah, yet not as sweet. More mulled."

Beth ladled up some submerged almonds and offered me a sip. It bit like nutmeg, but lingered on the palate. Velvety.

"Nice," I said, and she smiled.

"Say, what's with your friends?" she asked.

"Why?"

"There've been like three women in here since you left, spraying like cats. I'm not crossing any lines here, am I?"

Her tone sounded more bemused than anything. Both unthreatened and unthreatening.

"Not that I know of," I said.

Again she smiled, then resumed stirring. I found myself wondering about the "old friend" she'd come with, but didn't ask about him.

Towards dark the party dispersed, many of us heading into town for a Valentine's Day Reading two of the other guests were giving at a bookstore. Their repertoire offered no hint of Hallmark, though. One read a story about a bi-plane pilot who wrote fleeting love poems across the sky that fell to earth unrequited. The other admitted having hoped to share a love story, yet every time he tried to write one, they ended in violence. Sitting in the back row, I felt the day's wonderland seeping away.

Drinks at a nearby bar followed, and eventually I found myself alone and drunk in a corner booth. Well, not exactly alone. A couple other pitiful souls leaned against the bar rail, the kind you'd expect to find alone on Valentine's. The night seemed to be going on and on without any end in sight, drowning any remnants of the sun-filled day. Everything around me started to reverberate in red—the jukebox lights, the blood-colored walls, the desperate dregs of my last-call pint. Well, here you have it, I thought. Your blessed solitude. Drink it up.

Luckily I managed to drive home safely. No way, however, could I finesse the ladder up to my loft bed. I fell into the rocking chair and stared at the unblinking phone machine. No messages. No red pulse. Not a one. It was everything I could muster not to telephone New York and at least hear Sybil's voice.

Instead, I dialed my sister.

"Jesus, it's almost three," she said. "Are you all right?"

"Oh yeah. I just been driving, and wondering ..."

There was a space on the other end of the phone. This wasn't something I'd ever done—not with my sister, or anyone else for that matter.

"Where do you put it?" I asked.

"You're drunk, aren't you?"

"Yeah," I tittered. "Yeah … where do you put it?"

"Put what?"

"The love. The love from when you were married?"

Another silence rose between us. This one longer, deeper.

"I don't know what you're asking, but I don't think I'd call it that anymore. More like a dull anger. Anger and lingering lawyer bills."

"Yeah, okay. But there *was* love there once, right? Admit that."

" … Yeah, so?"

"So where did you put it? I mean, physically. Where did you put it in your body?"

I was picturing the times I'd come visit them in their big grey house with its white picket fence and toddlers, and how each time I couldn't imagine ever having anything like that. Picturing the night I'd sat in a car outside and watched my soon to be ex-brother-in-law folding laundry in an upstairs window. Sitting there idling by the curb, and wondering where and how their marriage went off track.

"You're not making any sense," said my sister.

"Sure I am. Perfect sense. Where do you attach that love now that you're apart? Where do you put it?"

"Look, why don't you go to sleep and in the morning—"

"NO! No. I want an answer," I said. "Please."

Again, a space.

"You're not going to like it."

"Where?" I said.

" ... Somewhere else. You pack it away somewhere else, like in a box or a closet. Both that love and then even the memory of it."

I waited for more words, but none came.

"That's it?" I said.

"Yeah, that's it."

I could feel the receiver, blunt against my cheek. The chair, pressing at my back.

"But I can't do that. I'm ... too afraid," I said. The words just leaked out of me. I could hardly believe it.

"Afraid of what?" my sister said.

"Oh, I don't know. Forgetting maybe."

She chuckled. "Well, don't worry about that. That much I can guarantee, at least where you're concerned."

"What's that supposed to mean?"

"Oh c'mon, get real. You hold on to everything."

"No I don't."

"Sure you do, with a vengeance."

Outside the window, everything shone blue with moonlight. The deck, the pond, the pasture. The whole damn world.

"Is there snow by you?" I asked.

"Yeah, there's snow. Over two feet. But hey, I've got to get to sleep. Some of us have to get up in the morning, you know. Dress kids, go to work ..."

"Oh yeah, I'm sorry."

"...It's okay."

It was time to hang up, but I held on.

"I wasn't much help when you were divorcing, was I?"

A thousand miles away, I could hear my sister breathing.

"No, you weren't," she said. "But neither was anybody else, really. In the end it's just yourself who's got to deal with it...Now why don't you try and get some sleep, okay?"

"Okay..."

18 February. Lots of catch-up. Sudden gaps in this diary. Too busy with schoolwork and socializing of late—readings, brunches, a Mardi Gras party. And, believe it or not, a date! Yeah, amazing what's out there, once you leave yourself open to it. Just a movie with a classmate, but then she suggested I stay over. It was late, the roads icy...so, this morning waking in her bed, lying close yet not touching. Wanting to go further last night, yet too unsure to take the next step. Too wary. When she awoke she smiled and headed off to the bathroom, her footsteps padding across the floor. Her hair long and curly. Echoes from New York. Remembering, yet not wanting to remember. Outside the window, more snowfall. Someone shoveling. A barking dog. And me just wanting to get back out to Redbird. Back to my safe little sanctum. My sanctimonious little...

Lucky I held the Valentine's party when I did, because within the week I lost water at the schoolhouse. Broken plumbing—

the irony not entirely lost on me. Tina called me down to her home the following day to inform me it wasn't simply a frozen pipe as she'd first guessed, but a broken housing in the main well down by the barn. A far more serious problem not worth the expense for repair, since she'd now be selling the farm. She was very apologetic.

"What are you saying?" I said.

"Well, in all good conscience, I can't keep renting the place."

I stared at her, uncomprehending.

"You mean I have to leave?"

"Not unless you want to live without water."

20 February. Up at 7 AM, my bowels propelling me out into the woods. A real pain in the butt, so to speak. Imagine both my pairs of cheeks were turning red in the cold! But sort of refreshing. After all, people did this for centuries.

22 February. Morning squat like clockwork. Noted tracks around my piles from the past few days—a curious dog, or maybe coyote. Checking out my scat! Which, by the way, looks as if I could stand chewing my food a little better!

23 February. Need to get something up here to store more water. Say, a 50-gallon feed trough? Could fill it up with 5 gallon buckets down at Tina's spigot every couple weeks. No different than how I've been hauling up my drinking water by sled. Piece of cake.

26 February. Showered in town today at the Rec Center, first time in days. Noticed a few of the same faces, the handful of homeless, even in this small town…Letter from Mom today with a clipping about some old holdout farmer. She highlighted one quote: "Sure we have running water. We run outside and get two pails full and run back." Should write back telling her how I boiled a pot full of snow to wash my dishes this morning. As long as winter holds, I can conserve even more water. Don't need plumbing, toilet paper, nothing. Fuck civilization. I don't need no-thing and no-body.

Last of February. Phone message today. Beth, inviting me to a dinner party. I'm almost tempted, but have a story to finish for class, and two squirrels in the fridge to skin out... Backpedaling, I know. Got to fight this rabbit instinct.

That same night, I was awakened from a deep sleep by another call. The voice on the phone sounded far away, foreign.

"Alessandro?" I whispered.

"*Si.*"

"Is that you?"

"*Si, sono io.*"

"Where are you?"

"*Cosa?*"

"*Dové sei?*" I said.

"*Ah, qui* a San Francisco."

I squinted at the orange-faced alarm clock. It was late, even in California.

"*Poi richiamarmi?*" he asked.

"What?"

"Can you to call me back? Here is number... "

Everything seemed askew, as if part of a dream. Even the telephone number he gave me was strange. I turned on a lamp, put on my glasses, and dialed him back.

"What number is this?"

"*Un ufficio.*"

"An office. What office?"

"Oh, this guy. He is letting me to stay here."

"What are you talking about, Aless? You're not making any sense."

As it turned out, a friend was letting him sleep on a couch in his office so long as Aless was up and out by 8 AM. In the month since we'd last spoken, Alessandro had lost all his part-time cooking jobs save one. He couldn't pay his rent and was kicked out of his apartment.

"What about Lua?" I asked.

He didn't respond.

"Aless?"

"I can't call her no more."

"Why not?"

"I can't. Okay! Don't ask me this!"

"Okay. Okay. Calm down. *Calma ti.*"

The line connecting our voices suddenly seemed very long and thin. I could barely hear his faint exhales.

"And your AZT?" I asked.

"Yes. I have still the pills."

"And food?"

"Yes. I get soup from kitchen."

His voice was settling down again, if still shaky. I gave him some advice for landing jobs and a new place to live. Asked him about those Venetian masks he'd been making the last time we spoke. He laughed.

"Already I tried this," he said. "I sold only one to a Pizza man from Napoli. No, in America nobody has need to buy masks. They already have. A whole parade on the streets every day, no?"

I couldn't respond to that. Instead, I spoke to him in Italian about the past. About Venice and the canals and Carnivale. I spoke until I got a true laugh out of him. At the time, it seemed the best I could offer.

"You stay in touch, okay?" I said.

"*Si.*"

"Promise me."

"*Si. Ti giuro.*"

His voice was cracking, growing faint. I had to say something, and fast.

"And call collect," I added.

But he'd already hung up.

In the morning I realized Aless wasn't talking about getting soup from the kitchen where he worked, but about Soup Kitchens—my friend, my brother, out on the streets and hungry. I drove into town to arrange wiring him cash. A mere hundred dollars, but it was all I could spare. Part of me knew I should be doing more, sending him an airline ticket to Iowa or going out there myself.

8 March. Day of the Woman. Remembering everyone in Venice with their little fistfuls of yellow mimosa blossoms as gifts. How one year I taped one to a postcard and mailed it to Sybil...Anyway, a break in the weather today. Finally, some melting. Dialed my mother and sister and wished them my best. Thanked them even.

Also drove Tina into town for a dentist's appointment—a rare and humbling request for her to have made. Away from Redbird, she looked suddenly older and frailer. When the nurse called her in, she passed me her purse to hold, her hand unsteady... Sitting in the waiting room, it occurred to me that after seven months as neighbors we hardly knew a damn thing about one another. I really need to learn how to talk to people. Like I wonder how she must feel having to sell this place after 30 years. 30 years. How does one finally come to such a decision? Or more to the point, to act on it?

Music
Appreciation

2 March. Never mind yesterday's –5° windchill or last night's lullaby of flurries, overnight it's as if the whole world melted. You could literally smell the shift in the air this morning. Hear it too, in the syncopated dripping from the eaves, and the trill of the first redwing blackbird down by Lower Pond. A male, staking out his nesting ground … Spring, it's coming! Sat out on the deck in shirtsleeves. Almost forgot how good those warm rays could feel.

16 March. Nearly 1 AM. Lying here listening to a cassette by Arvo Pärt that Beth lent me earlier this evening. Yeah, I know, I know. Said I wouldn't go, but this was her third dinner invitation. And frankly, the evening was lovely. All candlelit and cloth napkins, a delicious fish and cilantro stew, and her other guests equally spicy and entertaining. Mostly dancers and actors, who seem much easier going than my other friends here. Far more present and in their bodies. Writers seem to live mostly from the neck up. I like Beth a lot, too. She's damn honest and direct. Smart, and pretty. And obviously she's not short of dinner guests, so I'm guessing there's a reason she kept inviting me. Yes, definitely something there …

Anyway, liner notes talk about Pärt's style—what he calls tintinnabulation—his compositions as reliant on their pauses as on their sparse tones. The silences resounding. "… music that just as it is about to die away, blooms with infatuation." Reminds me a little of Venice in the late afternoon, pausing on the bridge near Calle Lunga to listen to church bells. The wake of each knell receding into another until at some point you'd realize they'd long since stopped, and vespers already begun …

I recall reading somewhere that the blind can still logically orient themselves in space, but that for the deaf, at least in certain fundamental ways, the world refuses to make sense. That what goes unheard can create incomprehensible and unbridgeable gaps.

The next time I entered the woods, I sat down beneath a tree, closed my eyes, and didn't rush to identify each birdsong as cardinal or peewee or dove, but listened instead to the softer lulls between each call. And within mere minutes, I started to discern a larger harmony at work. Stunning—a whole system of communication in which each species awaited its respective turn to speak, not unlike the way cars merged among parallel lanes of flowing traffic.

I opened my eyes onto a naked tree branch trembling above me. It felt as if I'd suddenly unveiled some lost and unspoken language.

At the writing desk, too, I was learning to harness the power and poignancy of white space. What I'd always presumed as the private domain of poetry could also prove critical in rendering prose. Those overlooked spaces between scenes and paragraphs, sentences, words. Those breadths, and breaths.

Narratives, after all, were compositions. They needed not only find their right rhythms, but proper pitches and tones and meters. Reciting my sentences aloud, I could feel them emerging between breaths, and sometimes I'd tap them out on the balls of my feet while pacing about the room. After all, weren't stories journeys, moving us through time and space? Dimensional in design? A kind of dance then. A choreography of characters...scenes...perspective...

19 March. Locked up the gate today so no one mistakenly drives up here. The gravel's all spongy and Tina says it could be another month or two till it fully dries. So, for the time being still need to haul up my water and groceries by hand. Meanwhile, my winter's worth of shit is starting to decompose into the woods' floor. More fertilizer for the coming wildflowers. Moss already showing orange sprouts. A whole subterranean world of change going on right beneath me. Upper Pond's ice floe has receded a good 25 feet from the southern bank. Strange, ten days ago I walked across it, listening for its deep thunders.

Later. The 20th, now. 2:30 in the morning. Stayed in town after class tonight, talking with Beth on her porch for an hour or so. About all kinds of things. She's so easy to talk with, so direct and open. Kept feeling myself leaning forward and engaged, then back against the wicker chair, thinking I shouldn't be there. But why not, because of Sybil? Still? Anyway, went to the bar afterwards to play eight ball with a few classmates. Noted the scattering of balls against the felt, the bumping of bodies on the dance floor, the cornmeal the barkeep sprinkled underfoot to keep us from slipping. The Clash. Mack the Knife. Zorba the Greek. What a GREAT jukebox! What fun to spend every penny in your pocket and close down the place. To let loose again…

21 March. Spring's officially sprung, yet fresh snow lay on the ground this morning. Only an inch or so. Bizarre, this weather. Unnatural. Yesterday a sudden hailstorm around noon, then 50° by sunset. Then this morning, witnessed a snowflake fall onto open water and refuse to melt. It's as if winter is defying the calendar, clutching tight to its mittens and scarves, its kindling and maul. Me too, I guess, still choosing barbed wire for neighbors. My hermit's pose still holding strong. My distances. But meeting Chris for an equinox walk out in the Amanas today…

"So, how goes it with the dancer?" he asked.

The afternoon sun reached halfway down the ridge Chris and I were descending.

"Okay, I guess. We seem to connect," I said.

"Meaning?"

"Oh you know, talking and stuff. She's pretty damn insightful. I always feel like I'm learning something with her."

"And she from you?"

"Yeah," I said. "Yeah, I think so. Different things."

We'd been hiking about half an hour. Below us the creek bed trickled with the day's melt, though patches of white still hunkered down in the draws.

"So what's the problem then?" he asked.

"There is no problem," I said.

"So then what're you waiting for?"

"I don't know ... I guess she's just not my type."

Chris paused to face me.

"What the fuck's that supposed to mean?"

I glanced toward the ground. My boots were all caked with mud.

"Oh you know," I said, "physically.

He exhaled and looked off to the north.

"Physically, or historically?"

"Meaning, what?"

"Meaning your ex in New York."

Chris had met Sybil the previous year when she'd visited.

" ... Both," I said.

"No, choose one," he said.

Now I paused. He was right. Beth didn't look anything like Sybil. Lighter skinned and lighter haired, her locks dyed a deep red and cropped short. Her clothes more loose fitting than tailored. So yes, a whole different kind of physicality, but beyond that a different temperament as well. A whole different orientation toward the world and way of communicating. Beth and I didn't need to go or do anything when we were together. Talking seemed exotic enough.

I exhaled. "Okay. Historically."

"Well then that doesn't mean squat."

"Sure it does."

"No. It doesn't," he said. "She's the one standing in front of you now. That's all that matters."

Chris walked past me and I watched him hop from one stone shelf to the next, down toward where the ground finally leveled off. The creek banks were narrow and littered with downed trees, some of which formed natural bridges. He stopped before one to inspect its peeling bark then stooped to pick up a rock with both hands.

"Look," he said straightening, "you said you're attracted to Beth, right?"

"Right, but—"

"But what?"

He stared at me then lay the stone up onto the fallen oak's span.

"It's not that easy, Chris."

"Who said it was gonna be easy?"

"You ... you're married, got kids and—"

"And you think *that's* easy?"

"No, but—"

"You think I didn't have a history? That my wife didn't have a history?"

"No, but—"

"But what? What?!"

Again he stared me down. Brown and white plumes stuck out from the daypack at his hip. A trove of hawk feathers we'd stumbled onto earlier. I searched their patterns.

"How old are you again?" Chris asked.

My birthday was in a week, but all I said was, "Almost thirty-three."

"So?" he said. "Tick tock."

He turned and headed upstream. Sunlight touched the brim of his bobbing hat and those feathers at his hip.

"C'mon, the mounds are waiting. It's getting late."

He crossed and re-crossed the tiny creek, choosing his footing among the mud and snow and rock. I caught up to him at the next impasse of tree trunk, where he again balanced a flat stone on its bridge.

"Hey, what's with the rocks," I called out.

"I like to leave them for the next time I come," he said. "To see what's changed. That'll happen, you know, whether you're there or not."

He wiped his palms against his thighs, then stared at me dead on.

"And not making a choice is still a choice, you know."

22 March. Well, the boxelder bugs are back. Out in droves on the windowpanes. Robins too, down in the thickets, and think I glimpsed a flash of bluebird near the upper pasture at dusk. Water levels are up a good foot on the ponds. Turkeys clucking each morning, but haven't seen one yet. Tina says they're about to "harem up," so is walking her dogs on leashes these days. Still no news from her regarding the sale. No phone messages from Alessandro either, but a couple from Beth. Wish she'd just leave me alone for a while.

23 March. If a man steps into the woods and no one hears it . . .

24 March. Was lying out under a tree again today, listening. Beyond the birds, beyond the silences. Beyond all those unheards and unspokens. Started wondering what kind of music lay inside me? What notes, what rests? What question?

More liner notes from Arvo Pärt:

> *"Time and timelessness are connected. This instant and eternity are struggling within us, and this is the cause of all of our contradictions, our obstinacy, our narrow-mindedness, our faith and grief."*

25 March. The last of the ponds relinquished its ice today. No snow left either, not even in the draws. Just like that. One day here, the next gone. Tossed a pebble and watched the concentric rings spread out on the water. Time. Movement. Sybil. Beth . . . learned she too is on the rebound, her last relationship particularly hurtful. So no wonder we're both hesitant, slowly circling one another . . . Nearly 1 AM now. Got Arvo Pärt playing again. This CD called Tabula Rasa. Outside, fires smolder on the horizon. Farmers burning back ditches. Returning geese eclipsing the moon . . .

27 March. The date alone should suffice. My birthday... And here I am, waking up at Beth's. She's in her kitchen brewing us coffee. Ruffled signs of her still among these sheets. The sun sifting through her lace curtains. The day, part dawn, part afterglow. It's nice here, scribbling away on paper scraps. So soft and warm. Nest-like... What was it I wrote recently—overnight, the whole world melted—yeah, feels just like that. New surfaces sprouting. New bodies. That old silken touch of skin, yet different. Beth's strong, able to actually lift me from below... How could I have forgotten, and why HAVE I waited so long? Or maybe the bigger question is why Beth? I don't know, I guess I finally decided enough was enough. It was my birthday. Why NOT Beth? Maybe that's the bigger question. After all, here you are waking up in HER home. That certainly could never happen with Sybil.

I'd previously planned a small gathering at the schoolhouse for later the same day. A sort of anonymous birthday party, since no one invited knew. To celebrate spring, I'd told them.

Around midday everyone came toting their potluck dishes, and the afternoon stretched long and lazy with shared woodswalks and food and talk. Toward dusk, however, Chris and his family unveiled a burning cake, which he set out onto the schoolhouse's stone table. Before shutting my eyes to blow out the candles, I noted many a chiding stare from around the room. Not least of which was Beth's.

"Today?" she said, cutting herself a slice of cake.

I nodded, figuring okay that's it. I blew it. She'll be out the door as soon as she finishes her last forkful.

"And none of these people knew?" she asked.

"I thought not."

"But they're your friends, right?"

Her brow was creased. The serrated knife still in her hand, poised in the air between us. Thankfully, she looked more puzzled than angry.

"Right," I answered. It was all I could muster.

Beth set the knife back down on the tabletop. Along with her slice of cake, she seemed to be chewing her thoughts.

"Interesting," she finally said. "…but was there any particular reason you didn't share this info with me last night?"

"Okay, so how'd you know?" I asked Chris.

He raised a single eyebrow and pulled me over to one corner of the room.

"Sybil," he said.

I stared at him.

"She called a couple days ago. Remembered my name from last year, must've gotten our number from information. Anyway, said she'd send a check to cover for the cake."

I was having difficulty gathering his words.

"But, why you?"

"Cause we bought the cake."

"No, why—"

"I know, I know. Lighten up, will you?" he said. "And don't try to turn this onto me. You're the one who wasn't answering your phone."

I stood there gazing over his shoulder. Out past the wash of voices in the room and the questions in Beth's eyes. Out someplace beyond the pond and the pasture. The present, the past.

"Here, have some cake," said Chris smiling. "You can thank me later."

He jabbed a plastic fork at my chest. Beneath my shirt I could feel the tiny pricks of its tines converging.

Across the room, Beth was talking with another guest. She hadn't left, at least not yet. When the telephone rang, I nearly jumped. The call wasn't from New York, though. Just California. Lua. I couldn't hear what she was saying amid the party, so retreated into the bathroom and closed myself in.

"Now, what's this?" I said.

"It's Aless," she said. "He's in San Francisco General. They found him collapsed on the street."

"What? I just talked to him."

"When?"

"I don't know. A couple weeks back."

"He's blacked out three times this past week."

Beyond her voice I could hear a metallic tone, doctors being paged. Beyond my bathroom door, laughter. I sat down on my toilet, the first time in over a month, I realized.

"But how did they find—"

"His wallet," said Lua. "My number was still in it."

"Oh. Right," I said. "And, so, what …"

"Well, right now he's still in the ER. They're running more tests. Last I heard they think he's lost some peripheral vision …" Lua's voice started to crack. "Oh, by the way, sorry to dump this on you on your birthday."

Again I heard a swell of laughter outside. Across from me the shower stall was coated with rust. The sink's basin all chalked over with neglect. Everything around me felt broken and useless. Suspended.

"Jesus," I said to Lua, "This is it, isn't it?"

I waited for her answer, but none came. In that vacuum of silence I could hear it all. My heartbeats. The humming of the world. Everything.

Lost And Found

❧

Some mornings you wake to find everything feels upside down. The rules of gravity you've lived by suddenly undone. You've lost count of the date, forgotten who you are. Or why. Or maybe you neglected to remind yourself the night before, so when daylight came you'd know what to do. Know to push the bed covers to the mattress' edge and begin, once again …

Another unanswered phone call to Lua last night. Another goddamn answering machine. Shoe's on the other foot now, huh? But this waiting is driving me crazy. This weather! Day to day the thermometer bounces up and down like a yo-yo. The hillside greens, only to wilt back in confusion. Nothing's making sense anymore. Not even this journal. Everything, upside down.

Dawn. April first, the Day of Fools. I glance out my window to yet another blanket of white. Part of me longs to roll back over into the sheets, to simply bury my head from this rollercoaster of weather and emotions. And yet with a fresh snowfall comes a glimpse, at least for the moment, that you can still start over. That the whole world had been mercifully whited out while you slept, offering total erasure. No past, no future, no references whatsoever.

I stepped out of the schoolhouse and happily strode into such oblivion thinking maybe it was true. Maybe I could just lose myself out here entirely. Disappear. At the bottom of the hillside, however, I turned and saw my dark footprints clearly marking the earth behind me. I pictured the tiny imprints of infants—not yet an hour old and dipped in ink then pressed onto a sheet of white. Our first steps ever, soiled. Incredible. What absolute messes we make of ourselves.

1:30 AM Can't sleep. Can't read. Can't call anyone, too late, too early. Guess I'll just write. What else is new? What's ever new with me? This day-to-day recording of events—makes me wonder what it all adds up to. Why I even bother. Guess I can write about the pair of Canada geese nesting at the edge of Woods Pond. About how the female sits hour after hour, while the male patrols the water. Or about how the spillway was overflowing this morning. Or how Jim Walters stopped by today to set up new bluebird houses, experimenting with slotted entrances this Spring vs. round holes. I can write that detail down. Or how he told me his father is still feeding off of Paige's frozen meals. How the whole family received posthumous mail order gifts from her at Christmas. Now there's an intriguing tidbit worth saving. A story worth co-opting, fictionalizing.

Or maybe I should just stop avoiding what else transpired today. About finally hearing from Lua and how all the test results are in and how we now have precise names for what's happening to Aless' body. Toxoplasmosis. PML. There. There they are. Written down and duly documented. Unretractable now. Undeniable facts. And I guess in the next sentence I can go on to explain their meanings and symptoms, their consequences. I can go on and on till kingdom come, till hell freezes over, till the goddamn cows come home . . . but I'm tired of words and of naming every damned thing. I'm sick and I'm tired, tired even of the melodrama I'm making of it all. All I want to do now is sleep.

At the bottom of the hillside I left my dark footprints behind and hopped the fence into the pasture, where hoof prints dotted the pale ground, the bottomland already running muddy. April Fools indeed—winter's refrain wouldn't even last the morning.

I climbed to the pasture's crest and ducked between the barbs of the fence line into the 60-Acre Woods. Before me rose a grove of locust trees, their thick thorns circling each trunk, maroon and threatening. On the ground lay a rusted leaf among the snowy mulch, a pin oak's. It probably fell months ago, yet its many points were still intact, the under-stem retaining its gentle arc. How did such fragile things manage to survive the elements?

Soon the ridge flattened into floodplain. Ice-snapped branches littered the path, thousands of dislodged red buds scattered underfoot that would now never blossom. Ahead curved the north branch of Old Man's Creek, the water high and running, a neighbor's untilled field beyond. I'd come about as far as I could go.

I turned and started heading upstream. On the opposite bank lay a half-buried Chevy from the 1950s, as if kneeling in the mud praying, one passenger door splayed out for support. On the near bank loomed the young mulberry tree, beneath which lay that shot deer's remains from December. I hadn't visited since the day Tina told me about having to sell the schoolhouse. Here I was, back to my old haunts and habits again. My obsessive circling. My endless partnering with the past.

Saturday. April whatever. The days slipping by. A strand of lost hours, unraveling with or without me. Oh my, aren't we poetic—a necklace of time. Jesus, why don't you just choke on it. Isn't there a point where you finally grow disgusted with your own wallowing? Like last night, drunk and barreling down Black Diamond, wringing the steering wheel for all it was worth, speeding past Old Man's Creek and Redbird's mailbox and, where was I going anyway? Nowhere, that's where ... I'd been at a party. One of those desperate start-to-say-goodbye-gatherings that seem to be popping up like so many wildflowers now that the school year's dwindling. My classmates all smiles and celebration when what no one will admit is how inconsequential we feel. How scared that within weeks we'll graduate and disperse. Move on. Just like that ... There's no community here, nothing but a college and a hospital. Degrees and Disease, that's all. A carousel of patients and transients ... The sky a flat grey today. The distant pasture emptying. Andre took two more to auction last week—Sokol and Rosa—the team who'd pulled us on our sleigh rides. Rosa, whose compliant back offered me riding lessons. Soon all the horses will be gone—Tina not renewing his lease either ... Still no word on the sale ... Outside, the wind's relentless, the schoolhouse walls whining like cats. Like me. Enough already!

I stood up from checking the deer's carcass and walked over to the creek to wash off my hands. The water was biting cold and I quickly dried them against my coat. Across the way ran a long fence between two fallow fields, its cedar posts leaning into the wind. A quarter mile off some colored fabric fluttered on its barbed wire. A mislaid farmer's cap? A shred of clothing? I thought about what Tina once said, how you never truly belonged to a place until you buried one of your dead there.

I glanced back toward the mulberry tree. No, no more. *Basta!* Time for the living now. Daylight was burning and I needed to get back to the schoolhouse and make a few phone calls to help Lua in San Francisco. To deal with the now and the next. With realities, not fictions. Hotlines, Crisis Centers, Medicall, Hospice. Inside, I felt empty and utterly parched. I scooped a handful of fresh snow from the bank—the first bite tasteless, the second no better. I closed my fist around what remained and dropped it into the thin current. The white ball floated like a tumor in the dark water, bobbing downstream toward Old Man.

18 April. Okay, a date. Time to get back on the stick again… While in Windam today for groceries, heard the official word—yesterday's flurries will be the last. Always interesting listening to farmers talk about weather. They'll report it, pray on it, stand helpless and cussing at its feet, but never complain like city folk. Seems those who stand to lose the most, who take on REAL risk, they don't whine when things turn south. Nope, they quietly endure. Actually no, they adapt… and move on.

Finally Spring arrived, and with a vengeance. First, the curly hairs of hepatica pushed through the last few patches of snow, and within days the woods' floor became a spreading palette of petals colored lavender, white, and yellow. Bellworts and violets, Dutchman's britches, anemone. Then came scarlet cup mushrooms, burgundy trilliums, nearly any hue you could imagine. Soon I was filling my nostrils and arms alike. I gathered young dandelion leaves to spice up my salads, sprigs of curly dock and nettle tips to steam with splashes of lemon. Then one day, I heard someone whispering about another delicacy sprouting in the woods. A mushroom called morel.

Some say they arrive when the bluebells first bloom. Or when young oak leaves get about the size of squirrel ears. Some say they favor northern slopes, others western. Some swear morels hide under mayapples, others near dead elms, and still others flanking young moss. Some wield divining rods before them like the blind, others tote lucky talismans in back pockets. As far as I could tell, every mushroom hunter had his own opinion as to *how* to find morels, but not a single one would divulge precisely *where*.

Tina was kind enough to show me what one looked like, holding out its odd honeycombed head and squat stem in her palm.

"That small, huh?"

"Some," she said.

"I thought they were supposed to be flesh-colored?"

"That's another species, the yellows. This one's a grey. It's more rare and pungent. You'll only find these for a few more days. The yellows will follow and last a couple weeks, depending on the heat and rain. But that's it. Not much of a season for slackers."

"Where'd you find this one?" I blurted.

She stared at me as if I were even worse than a slacker.

"Can't answer that, can you?"

"Nope," she said, and started walking away. "They're out there though. You just have to look for them."

I started out haphazardly glancing at the slopes and stands nearest the schoolhouse. Once I spied a couple of the greys, it was like I got sprayed with magic fairy spores and turned into a little child again, darting about on a secret scavenger hunt. I began hugging old fence lines and combing through the spreading bloodroot and Virginia creeper. I foraged as close to the ground as a chipmunk, rubbing jewelweed on my forearms to counter any poison ivy. After awhile, I began to spot morels where there weren't any—their twisted forms and leaning heads surely hiding beneath the next leaf.

Come evening, I'd spill my cache onto the stone tabletop then arrange two buckets of water for their washing. I sliced each mushroom lengthwise and stripped tiny slugs from their bellies, squadrons of spilled ants duly commandeering the schoolhouse floor. But it didn't matter. I had my morels. Lightly sautéed in olive oil and black pepper, they dripped with a flavor as thick and enchanting as smoke.

26 April. The schoolhouse hill a deep green now, almost blue come dusk. Bats suddenly wheeling in mid-air about the roof, blind and ravenous. Young ivy climbing up the clapboard. And in the woods—Spring beauties and Jack-in-the-pulpits, mayapples unfurling like tiny patio umbrellas. Another big birding day, too. Saw my first osprey ever at Upper Pond. And glimpsed a whole flock of white pelicans, miles and miles up there. The fleeting glint of their wings catching the sun, then they'd bank and disappear, then reappear like magic.

2 May. Finally spoke with Aless tonight. Everything's set for him to go back to Italy. Lua arranged it all with his brother and sister, who finally told their parents. Part of me regrets this move. San Francisco's probably the best place in the world for him to be medically, but guess it's better he's back home with family. Real family who'll look after him now. Plus there's an HIV clinic about an hour or so away in Portogruaro... Yeah, Lua did the right thing. The decent thing too, given all that's between them. Stepped up to do what was needed... Aless sounded okay on the phone. A little weak, maybe. Frightened.

Late one morning, I came back from mushrooming to find my professor sitting outside the schoolhouse. As it turns out, James Alan McPherson was an old friend of Tina's, and had come over for a tea with her on the schoolhouse deck. Over the course of the semester, my admiration for him had grown. In a heartbeat, he'd shift from an almost painful shyness to an irreverent humor, telling off-color jokes or quoting the Bible to help prove a point—risky things in these lean years of political correctness in the academy—yet always remaining deeply vulnerable and giving.

I'd also responded strongly to his writings and teaching style. Our assigned reading list spanned the globe and several centuries, and his seminars were dizzying riffs on questions of ethics and race and community, of voiced pangs and hopes. His lessons on writing were different, not only about technique and grammar but about the crossroads of place and character, about owning your individual point-of-view. For McPherson, writing was all about context and accountability. For me, he'd become not only a teacher, but a moral compass.

"What's in the bag?" he asked as I approached.

"Lunch."

I extracted a couple of morels and set them on the deck rail. McPherson dipped his head to peer over his glasses.

"Strange looking mothers," he said.

"Yeah, they are, aren't they?"

"And they're safe to eat?"

"Better than safe, Professor McPherson."

I showed him the rest of my stash, naming each leaf and flower of the greens I'd gathered for a salad.

"You're really into this stuff, huh?" he said.

I looked up at him, then past his shoulder at the splashes of purple thistle on the hillside. On one perched a perfect goldfinch.

"Yeah," I said. "Yeah, I guess I am."

"Well, maybe you should write about mushrooms then. About this place."

His voice sounded both muted and mischievous. I gauged the slight curl to his lip, the warmth in his eyes.

"Well, I have," I admitted. "But only in my journals."

"That's okay. Grist for the mill. Grease for the pan."

"Oh, I don't know," I said. "I'm not so sure anymore. The more I document, the less I seem to know, or at least grasp. I mean, to tell the truth, lately I'd much rather just live it than record it."

McPherson chuckled.

"Well, there's that," he said. "There's documenting and then there's interpreting. The difference between what you find, and what you make of it. What you do about it."

The next afternoon, I invited Beth over for morel hunting and dinner. We'd been seeing each other now and then, and on occasion she'd sleep over. Our duet still felt a bit clumsy, but we were steadily revealing more confidences, sharing our pasts and our fears. I learned about her first marriage, and she about my struggles with Sybil. We talked about creative process too, about what it meant to try and make a dance, a story. We talked in ways I never could with anyone. She could even call me out without it feeling judgmental. Without my having to push back, or run for the hills.

Once she arrived, we headed out into the woods with our mushroom baskets in arm. I led us to a couple reliable spots nearby before we hiked up into the 60-Acre woods. Among the thinner trails we found bountiful new patches and stunning wildflowers to boot. Beth's favorites were columbines, mine the shooting stars. When our baskets were half-full of plucked morels, we sat down for a breather on a fallen tree trunk.

"It can get a little obsessive," I said.

" … Yeah."

Beth extended one leg and leaned out over it, then switched legs. Dancer stretches. I admired her work as a choreographer, that she spent time thinking about how bodies moved through space. As she leaned forward, her red hair brushed the ground.

"Oh, hey," I said. "I've been meaning to tell you. I was reading this essay on bees and they have this whole system of air dances they use for communication. Like, turning about in circles might tell how far away a field of clover is, or another movement might say it's time to feed a new queen, or move their hive. Pretty cool, huh?"

Beth came back up to a seated position. "Yeah," she said, then stared deep into her basket of mushrooms.

"You okay?" I said.

She lifted a morel into her palm, but still hadn't looked up.

"What're we doing here?" she asked.

"Gathering dinner."

"No, I mean what're we doing here? You and me?"

Now it was my turn to look away.

"Don't get me wrong," she said, "it's beautiful out here and ... and I adore everything you're sharing with me ..."

"But?" I said.

"But nothing. Look, I'm not pushing you here. I only wanted to know if you've been asking yourself that question, too."

"Well, sure but ..."

"But what?"

"I don't know. I mean, I guess I've been a little pre-occupied lately. You know, with school ending and this thing with Alessandro and ..."

"And Sybil? Yeah, well, we're all busy with our ... luggage," she said. "And I'll admit I've been dragging my feet here too, a little."

I caught her eye then. Hazel in this light. She was being kind. Her hesitations were nothing compared to my backpedaling. She blinked then leveled her gaze at me.

"I mean, do you really think you're going to find whatever it is you're looking for out here alone in these woods?"

To make a good risotto is a labor of love, a patient and painstaking process of stirring and waiting. As I slid our now sautéed and sliced morels into the steaming pot, I was picturing those lazy noontime meals I used to fix myself in Venice. Meanwhile, Beth was sitting out on the schoolhouse deck, nursing a glass of wine and enjoying the sunset. No doubt we each needed these few private minutes to regroup.

As the last of the broth disappeared, I tested the risotto's final consistency, then folded in fresh parsley and grated Reggiano. After plating equal portions, I drizzled on a touch of olive oil, and topped each with a garnish of plucked violet. Outdoors, the bowls were met with solemn oohs and aahs. I lit the table's candles.

"So, this must be your seduction meal," said Beth.

"My what?"

"Don't all single guys have one?"

"Not that I know of... So then what's yours, fish stew?"

"Worked on you," said Beth.

We smiled. It felt nice to flirt and joke, not to mention to cook for two. I refilled her glass and we calmly toasted the hillside and horizon. The thing about risotto, however, is once you get past the divine first forkful, you unwittingly slip into the mindless spooning of infants, and before you know it, you're scraping and squinting at bowl's bottom. All-gone.

High over our heads a few bats started circling with the dusk, gulping down their own dinners. Nature didn't pause much for manners or romance, did it? No, if there's anything I'd learned from the woods, it was that Nature was indifferent. Utterly blunt in its dealings, and blindly just. Nature didn't care a lick for the individual, didn't flirt or carry luggage. Didn't hesitate. Or apologize. It was all either eat or be eaten. Adapt or perish. One's thoughts or emotions were entirely irrelevant.

I looked up at Beth. I did feel something beyond mere pheromones and seduction between us, though. Did care a lot about her, and chanced telling her so. Flat out.

"And I like you, too," she said. "I wouldn't be here if I didn't sense any real potential."

I offered her the salad bowl. Then we each took turns dressing our greens.

"So now what?" I said.

"Well, at this juncture that's up to you, I think. Depends on whether you're really looking for something or running from it."

I glanced her way then out past the candlelight. Our backdrop showed silhouettes of grass and thistle. Shadows in the distance. Doubt.

"And here I was hoping you'd say dessert."

" … Case in point," she smiled.

On her plate lay an upturned fork, beside it peeked a violet blossom. I recalled the near hillside where I'd found my very first grey morel, and how the only reason why was because at the time I was looking for something else. What we stumble upon, another kind of grace.

"Look, I'm not here to take anything away from you," said Beth, "or force you into anything. Quite the opposite. This is all about choices here."

12 May. Fixed the barn's metal roof this morning. A couple sheets had blown clear off in the last storm. The paddock is overgrown now, too. I miss the horses and Andre. A couple gates are already sagging on their hinges. Abandoned tack, molding on the wall. Chris and McPherson and Beth are right—doing nothing IS a choice, with bitter consequences, too.

Later. The synchronicity, amazing. Got a letter from Sybil today. Well, not a letter, just a spare envelope containing a Xeroxed sheet of paper. No return address, not even any of her handwriting, though I can't blame her. I never mustered the courage to call her back after my birthday. Didn't even have the common decency to thank her for the cake. The photocopy she enclosed was a page out of a short story by J. California Cooper, one scant paragraph circled in red magic marker:

> *… he was a good man, a honest man, reliable, kind, sweet, always kept his word … BUT a person can think you good cause they don't know nothin bout you if you keeps your business to yourself! You can be honest, if you ain't poor and don't want nothing; new car, clean house, nothin! Reliable, if you don't promise nobody nothin but little bitty things don't take no time nor money, and kind, if you just smile and say nice things cause you ain't givin nobody nothing that would make you mad if you don't get it back. There was two sides to that coin and he was on both sides. Kept his word cause he never gave it if a thing was too big!*

Felt pretty angry after first reading it, but mostly at myself. Truth is she nailed that one right on the head. I didn't give much, did I? Not even my word. So, I can't rightly fault her for keeping herself distant either. Keeping her other life separate. After all, I wasn't offering her any alternatives. Any choices … meanwhile, this ongoing avoidance of mine has been much worse. More about not facing myself than not facing Sybil. Beyond cowardly. Heartless. Hurtful ...

14 May. 3 AM phone call from Tina—the switchgrass on fire down by her house! Rushed downhill to find flames ringing the marsh. A neighbor had seen it first and called the fire department. Tina was pretty shaken, mostly about not having awakened herself. The trucks came and put out the fire within an hour, but still. If the wind were different, it could've taken her house in minutes ... Sat with her afterwards, drinking tea till nearly dawn. Once or twice she looked like she might cry. Neither of us the hugging type, but it felt good sitting nearby, being there for her ... She confided a little about the land sale. Lots of complications and legal details causing delays. It seems certain I won't have to leave next month, but no way to project any date yet. I should feel relieved, but don't. Feels more like a stay of execution. I know, I know. Bring on the violins. This is hardly about me, but that's how I feel ... need to see it in its larger context, of changes, choices ... One thing for sure, if Tina had any doubts it was time for her to move on, this fire cured them. Said it was like a message. A burning bush in the night.

Weights and
Measures

え

The day after the marsh fire, a posse on horseback arrived at
Redbird—though not because of the fire. Each Spring, Tina
hosted a group of volunteer horsemen who worked as adjuncts
to the county sheriff's office. Mostly they aided with traffic
control at parades and public events, but sometimes were called
in on special criminal cases or manhunts. The day's outing at
Redbird was a chance to practice their search maneuvers.

Midmorning, I walked downhill and found the drive
flanked by pickups and hitched trailers. Strewn hay and horse

droppings led further downhill, where a long coffle of cowboys was bobbing toward the marsh across the road. Some sat astride mules, some were cowgirls, others children on Shetlands. Out ahead of them all was Tina on foot, angling toward the burn.

By the time I caught up with the pack, they'd already made a sweep of the charred switchgrass. Two of the front riders were huddled around a spot where the burn was darkest, one squatting on the ground. The other wore tinted eyeglasses and leaned out over his pommel.

"Yeah, I agree Tina. That's where she smoldered," he said.

The man on the ground didn't speak, rolling dark ashes between his fingertips. The air smelled stale. Part mud, part flame.

"Probably just a cigarette butt from a passing car," continued the first man.

"What about a tractor?" asked Tina.

The man on horseback squinted toward the ground and pursed his lips.

"Might could be," he said.

His partner slowly stood and gauged the distance from his boots to Black Diamond Road's asphalt. They exchanged a glance. The man on horseback's mount stirred and he tightened his rein.

"Any farmers round here smoke?" he said.

"Dozens," said Tina.

"Well, make us a list."

"No, that's alright," she said. "So long as I knew it wasn't set on purpose."

The second man dug his boot toe into the cinders.

"Nope. No arson here, ma'am. Just carelessness."

I stood off to the side, amazed at how a mere few minutes of observation on their parts had deftly narrowed down probable causes and culprits. In comparison, there I was, after all these months on Redbird taking notes and reflecting, still more or less in the woods. Still as mired in indecision as on the first day I'd arrived and fell in the mud.

At the university, I was feeling similarly frustrated and entrenched. The deadline for my thesis was fast approaching, yet I couldn't seem to gain any ground with revisions. Couldn't seem to let go of what I'd written in previous drafts. I made an appointment with one of the visiting professors, Margot Livesey. We met in her tiny office, surrounded by bulging bookcases and squared stacks of paper. Between us on the desk angled an excerpt from one of my drafts-in-progress.

"Now there's a difference, you see, between what's editing and what's real revising," she said, pointing at a marked paragraph in particular. "This here, this fussing with sentences and syntax you're doing, that's editing and should only come into play much later on in the process. Revision, frankly, is about seeing what isn't there yet."

I stared at my scribbled pages, trying to grasp what she was suggesting.

"Oh, and another thing. One of the first things I tell myself before sitting down to revise is that it won't be the last revision, which tends to take a little of the pressure off. Learning to tolerate our own mediocrity, that's often the hardest rub."

Still I sat there, no doubt squinting by now.

She exhaled, then smiled. "Look, revisions typically get worse before they get better," she said. "Sometimes it's about making small changes, sometimes about starting over fresh, taking blind leaps. Tossing out what you've initially presumed about your story. Or about your character ..."

19 May. Dug up a patch of grass beside the schoolhouse this morning for a garden. Have no idea what the hell I'm doing or if I'll even be living here for harvest, but at least I DID something tangible today. Brought up five wheelbarrows of old manure from the barn and planted tomatoes and peppers, zucchini and butternut, spinach and arugula. Measured out all the neat little spaces and depths, following directions for once. Time to get methodical again. "Iowa, A Place to Grow."

20 May. Woodswalk. Foraged the first wild strawberries and raspberries of the season. Plucked a good half-quart of each. Recent rains have been good. Basswood trees in bloom, purple asters, a rare showy orchis. Woods smelling sweeter than last month, heavy with phlox. Yes, a thinner, more subtle smell.

23 May. Landscape keeps changing at a tremendous rate. Hundreds of tadpoles sunning in the pond's shallows and cattails nearly thick as my pinkie finger. The last big thunderstorm downed two trees on the trail. Otherwise, spent much of yesterday in town. Met Beth for dinner. She bought me oregano and tarragon plants for my garden. Joked with me about my resistance to accepting gifts. Suggested I try resisting resistance for once. That one gave me pause. Plus, my fortune cookie read: A man of words and not of deeds is like a garden full of weeds.

Clearly the signposts were everywhere. The arrows all pointing toward change, urging me to let go of old habits and presumptions, to finally take action. To grow. Yet I still couldn't see it clearly, the greater pattern ahead still eluding me. My myopia stubborn as ever, weighing me down.

However, each Spring in the Midwest an undeniable miracle occurs. All across the landscape, as if by some invisible magnetic force, millions of tiny green dots start aligning themselves into straight rows. Row upon row. Acre upon acre. Corn.

I imagine for each farmer standing before his respective field, that moment feels no different than it must for the first-time father leaning with his palms against a maternity ward's window. His neck craned slightly forward, his bleary eyes searching the rows to first make sure what he's seeing is real, then taking a half-step back in awe, anticipating the work he must now shoulder to nurture and protect that seedling.

Of course only part of this equation is a miracle. The rest is machinery and math. Talking with Earlis Rohret down the road, he said arithmetic is probably the single activity that most occupies a farmer. His mind always generating numbers, tallying square acres and tractor hours, average rainfalls and mean crop yields. Frost lines and flood marks, quotes and futures. Gallons and tons, bushels, bales. I'd watched him seed his acreage back in early April, maneuvering his planter with delicacy and precision—sowing 28,000 seeds per acre, thirty-inch rows, seven-and-a-half inches between seeds. In his mind he'd mapped out his entire population, reckoning ears at sixteen kernels round and forty long, test weights tipping the scale at fifty-nine pounds per bushel. If X is his input, then Y should be his profit.

Most farmers, Tina told me, tend to financially kill themselves with optimism. In her estimation, Earlis was both a good and smart farmer because he took his worst season as his mean. Other neighboring farmers thought he'd planted too soon this year, but he'd done well to get an early start. Many who waited for the warm front got blindsided when the rains began.

Still, I imagined Earlis lying awake in bed at night, gleaning for what he might have overlooked. Factoring in forgotten liens and amortizations, principals and interest. Subtracting for headlands and busted fuel pumps and corn borers. Drainage. Droughts. Finally he'd fall off to sleep, more exhausted than worn, and it's little wonder he'd rise before dawn—work, a welcome relief from thinking.

Thinking, after all, never got anything done. It was all weight and no measure.

27 May. Clouds and showers today. Again. Along Black Diamond the best of fields are barely a foot high. Heard the bottomland's too wet to reseed. That it takes 5000 gallons of water to produce a single bushel of corn. Soy bean 13,000! Don't know how many gallons of rain it takes to ruin a bushel, but we must be getting close.

29 May. Another thunderstorm this afternoon. Another 8/10ths of an inch in my garden gauge. Bats in the attic squealing with the pressure change. Read how a single brown bat will consume half its own weight each night, as many as 600 insects per hour! They must fly with their mouths wide open ...

On either side of the schoolhouse's chimney peeked two slight gaps in the eaves from which the bats emerged each dusk. One evening I decided to take an actual count. I took my front row seat on the deck as the sun began sinking at around 8:45. Slowly the sky dimmed and down by the pond the bullfrogs began tuning their voices and then the lightning bugs ignited one by one. By 8:56 the chirping in the roof swelled and at 8:59 the first bat appeared.

At first they shot out sporadically, one at a time then in pairs splitting skyward like clay skeet pigeons. Eleven, twelve, seventeen, twenty-six, then a steady seamless stream. More hectic than a runway at LaGuardia, I thought, yet all perfectly silent. Most sped upward, others banked low and past my head. The hair on my forearms stood on edge. Bat after bat after bat—seventy-five, a hundred, a hundred and fifty, I could hardly keep up. By 9:35 the eaves trickled down to one or so every minute, the sky darting with their numbers. My final tally, three hundred ninety-two!

For three dusks running I monitored this northeast corner of the deck and arrived at an average of three hundred and sixty. Then I performed the same vigil at other gaps along the south and west eaves. All in all, I figured around eight hundred to one thousand bats were residing within the schoolhouse's roof. No wonder the deck was relatively mosquito free.

I telephoned Beth the next day to ask if she wanted to come out one evening and watch the bat show with me.

"I think I'll pass," she said.

"You sure?" I said. "It's perfectly safe."

"… That's not it, I'm kinda busy. You know? Starting work on my next concert."

I could discern something different in her voice.

"Beth?"

"Look, you just do what you want to do. You want to stay out there counting bats then fine, count your bats. But don't pretend like you're inviting me."

"I am inviting you."

"No, I mean *really* inviting me. Inviting me in."

I sat there with the receiver against my ear.

"I don't quite get what it is you're still carrying," she said, "whether it's this Sybil or, whatever. But hey, that's your choice … I'm just not going to do this to myself again. I'm not."

And then she hung up.

I stared at the phone. I should have redialed, but she was right—this was exactly what Sybil's letter said—I never truly risked anything personal. Nothing but little bitty things. The only reason Sybil and I lasted as long as we did was because we never pushed each other to be any more than what we already were. We stayed safe in our little cocoon, safely suspended, stunted. Whereas Beth was daring to ask more of me, more of us. Offering the very growth I'd supposedly wanted to find in Iowa.

6 June. Resist resistance. Maybe Beth's onto something… two negatives make a positive, right? So, how about denying denial, then? Avoiding avoidance? Abandoning loss?

Meanwhile, got a message on the phone machine today from Italy. The connection was bad, Aless' voice slipping in and out of static. Of sense. Something about pigeons and the right side of his body? I should call him back today, but can't. Just can't. Anyway, it's too late there now. Tomorrow maybe… I should have gone to see him in San Francisco. From that very first call. Gone and brought him back here. Should have weeded the garden today, too. The things I leave undone outnumber the done. The unsaid the said… Outside, heat lightning to the north. Rain coming, again. Eight nights running!

8 June. 5 AM. Cat caught in a flash of lightning, spread-eagle on the screen door, crying to come in from the storm. Had to literally pry her claws free. Again the sky flickers. Even with eyes closed I can sense the flashes.

12 June. This rain is ridiculous. It's starting to get almost biblical. "Dies Irae"… Pulled the plugs on all my clocks today. A desperate act? Maybe so. Started a letter to Alessandro but didn't get very far. Wound up getting sidetracked, staring at the rain, looking up "metaphor" in the dictionary. Its etymology from a couple of root words, meta (to change) and pherein (to bear, convey). So, a metaphor's not only about one object suggesting something else, but about associations that can bear the weight of change. Changes in perception, perspective. In critical mass. In character... there's that word again. Stories not only about setting and conflict and characters, but character.

A flood doesn't happen overnight. A neglected leak trickles down for days, sometimes weeks before you'll notice. The surrounding waters swell only an inch at a time and so you think you're still okay. Still safe and steadily treading water, your arms turning the same old circles—for months, sometimes years. And you keep telling yourself you'll never tire nor drown, that you can go it alone, wait it all out. You even begin to deny the part of you that's submerged.

Meanwhile there's a raft floating easily within reach, but you're stubborn. No, not stubborn. You're just too afraid. Too damn steeped in regrets.

By early July, the Mississippi was cresting. Dubuque already lay under water, Davenport flooding. All across Iowa—the Des Moines River, the Cedar, the Iowa—all of them, abandoning their banks. Residents in nearby Coralville were baling out their living rooms, businesses frantically stuffing sandbags. Iowa City's markets could hardly stock enough bottled water and concerns about sewage and hepatitis were rising. On July 7th, the governor declared Johnson County a State Disaster Area, and on the 10th, President Clinton bumped the status to

Federal. Within a few more days, Air Force One would land in Des Moines, like a doctor paying a house call.

Yet legislation does little to stop the flux of groundwater. Daily outflow figures from the local Coralville Dam continued to rise: 15,000 cubic feet per second ... 16,500 ... 19,000 ... 24,000. The Iowa River had climbed six feet above flood line. Old timers were recalling deluges of 1938, 1927, 1918 ... the dates, too, seeping back deeper to grandfathers and forefathers ... 1881 ... 1851 ...

At Redbird Farm, even tiny Old Man's Creek was affected. Neighboring cornfields wallowed in silt and, in some acreage, standing water. Farmers passed their days astride barstools, resigned to draining beers instead of fields. Even Earlis was already cutting his losses. Downhill, Tina's car was wading up to its wheel wells. Black Diamond Road impassable to the east, and what little asphalt remained visible lay littered with snakes and worms, puddles of tiny mosquito larvae, leopard frogs. Pretty soon we'd be counting plagues.

Up on the schoolhouse hill, however, I was safe. Perched high and dry above it all, yet with a steady sense of mounting unease. I could feel my whole stance, my whole carefully calculated world of distances slowly eroding beneath my feet. Face it, my days were an elaborate slough of avoidance: my garden unweeded, the zucchini swollen like melons on the vine, my water trough growing moldy, my dishes spilling out from their useless sink. My answering machine too was overflowing, but with no word from Beth, or Sybil. All the world over, water rose and water fell. Monsoons in Asia, *acqua alta* in Venice. I tried to picture Alessandro there, sitting before a window and watching the murky line between sky and water, waiting on his fate.

Inside my head and chest everything I'd been resisting was finally backing up and fast approaching a breaking point. I headed downhill and stole west on Black Diamond, detouring to find an open route into town. I wound up driving past the city park where I'd slept in my car upon first arriving in Iowa. From an overlook I could see its parking lot and baseball fields, all flooded. The Ferris wheel and carousel where I'd last seen Sybil, half under river water. Our circle of painted horses, stranded and adrift.

I drove on, eventually turning up breathless at Beth's front door. She answered my knocking, but didn't invite me inside. We sat on her porch instead.

"It's all crumbling away," I said. "Doomed."

She nearly laughed. "You're not doomed," she said.

"Not me, Alessandro."

She looked out past the porch rail. Across the street was a public park with lit street lamps. She took a deep breath.

"This is your friend in Italy, right? The one with AIDS."

"Yeah."

"Then I don't understand what you're waiting for. Go see him."

I sat there, silent. Once again, over-thinking. Weighing my words.

"Help me to understand you?!" she said. "Why?"

"Because I don't have the money. I don't…I don't know who I'd be going for more, him or me. It feels selfish."

"Of course it does. He's the one who's going to die. You'll just be the one left behind. How else should you feel?"

Above our heads a moth bounced against the porch light. Again and again.

"Look, it's like I already told you, you've got choices here. Which, quite frankly, is more than Alessandro has. No one else can do this for you, Marc. You want to wait until he dies to do something? You want to wait around till Sybil dies? Well be my guest, but to me it seems a hell of a way to live. Or, frankly, *not* live."

She was standing up now, heading for her door.

"You want to know what your real problem is? It's not that you're immature, it's that you've already grown old. And that's the worst of it. Wait around long enough, and you'll die, too."

17 July. Accidently hit a raccoon driving home from Beth's. Coming round that last curve on Black Diamond, suddenly two of them crossing the road. Couldn't swerve in time, swear I just clipped the second one. I felt so helpless, standing there over it, watching its fur balloon a little less with each breath. Then, finally, stop. I picked it up and started crying. Carried it back into the woods and lay it down on its side. I couldn't help thinking about its mate, watching us from the dark… Came home and wished I could dial Beth. Once again, she's right. There's got to be more to life than just surviving. Than just treading water…

One morning around this same time, Tina knocked on my door and asked if I could come out onto the deck to talk. Her voice was toned down a notch and I figured my final eviction date had arrived. Instead, she only requested I make myself scarce the following day for a few hours. A memorial service was being held on the property to commemorate the thirty-year anniversary of her daughter's death. She said she hoped I wouldn't mind. If it were up to her I'd be more than welcome, but there were others involved. In a rare moment, her eyes dropped, then she said she hoped I'd understand.

I had heard stories about her daughter. About a car accident in which two young girls, best of friends, were killed in the back seat. About Vance driving and surviving the wreck. About how quickly and irrevocably lives could crash. Entire families, futures. What I hadn't heard, though, was that the girls' ashes had been buried in the schoolhouse woods without any funeral or markers. As if it never happened.

The next morning, I helped Tina and her family set up chairs in a slight clearing she'd made in the woods. Her son Philip was there with his own son. Vance had come up from Louisiana, too. While nothing distinguished the spot from the surrounding trees, I figured this was the site of the burials. Tina approached me and said that since yesterday she'd spoken with the other girl's family and I could stay if I wanted, but I declined. If there was one thing I'd learned out here, it was that the grieving deserved their own space.

I drove into town and passed the day walking among people. People on sidewalks, parking their cars, carrying briefcases, having lunches. Bankers and mailmen and students by the dozen, young mothers pushing strollers. A whole bustling town and community I'd mostly chosen to shun. Along the river, piles of sandbags were being removed from around the water treatment plant and cliff swallows once again flitting beneath the bridges. The worst of the flood had passed, and lives were moving on.

I thought about Tina, stoically walking past that burial plot in the woods each and every morning for the past thirty years. I remembered bumping into her one day as I emerged from a deer run above Upper Pond. We walked side by side on the main trail until coming to the next major fork in the path, where I began to veer off again. Tina paused for the barest moment, as if to come along, then continued on her typical route, alone.

"So much in life is apprehension," I remember her once saying. "Far too much."

Thirty years, I thought. My God.

Then I thought about Tina's choosing to finally move on from this site. Or at least, this shrine. I recalled the story she'd shared about her grandfather, packing up all his belongings at seventy-nine years young for yet another frontier. Then I thought about my own grandfathers, the one who lived with bitter regrets, the other who'd succumbed to his. Was this what Beth kept alluding to about choice—my holding on not only being about past loss, but lost potential?

22 July. Paused on the berm alongside Lower Pond today, recalling the first time I took out its rowboat. Just learned the line of olive trees that flanks this stretch was planted by Tina and Vance back when their children were small. No fruit was ever expected to grow this far north, nonetheless they were planted. Their leaves now svelte and shiny, a gift to behold ... Tina recently presented me with Annie Dillard's book, "The Writing Life," which on page 68 advises:

> *"Write as if you were dying. At the same time, assume you write for an audience consisting solely of terminal patients. That is, after all, the case. What would you begin writing if you knew you would die soon? What could you say to a dying person that would not enrage by its triviality?"*

The phone call from Italy literally came the very next morning. Alessandro's mother told me they'd received my letter, in which I'd suggested coming to visit before Christmas. Perhaps early autumn, I'd written, when Aless and I could walk along the canals and stop in at his favorite *taverne* for the newly harvested wines. She said they'd read it to Aless and he'd smiled.

"What do you mean, read it to him?" I asked in Italian.

She inhaled awkwardly, and then I heard the sound of a chair scraping against the floor. Then the voice of Alessandro's younger sister.

"I don't know how to say you," she stuttered, "*Ma, Alessandro sta male. Molto male. È gia ... cieco.*"

"Blind?" I said.

"*Sì,*" she said. "He is blind."

222

I hung up the receiver. Then without pausing to think, I dialed the airlines.

What I Did On My Summer Vacation

❧

First of August. I am walking, but it is not me. It is memory walking. Memory leading my limbs through these twisting calle as if it were only yesterday. As if it weren't only two hours since I landed, two years since I last searched these stones for a pattern, a path. This is how time works— one foot in front of the other, one breath after another—passage. There is no other choice, is there? One may only advance by degrees here. You never can tell what's around the next corner, must rely on something beyond your eyes ... Up ahead, the stalls of Rialto, empty crates stacked along the fondamenta. The smell of fish, cheeses. A shopkeeper nods at me.

The one who used to sell me my asiago and gorgonzola, my mascarpone. He remembers, too. Steps back for the moment, riddles his brow. Winks at the world moving on with or without us. At the streets and the tides, the carrots, the onions... Venice. La Serenissima. Thousand year empire. Refuge from the Huns. Shimmer floating between sea and sky. Half mirage, half awash in dreams. Yet even here, in this shrine of a city, there is a date. A clock steadily ticking. Even here ...

For two days straight I walked the streets and bridges half-dazed by the brightness and swelter, the mass of moving bodies. Though all told I'd lived in Venice for nearly three years, I'd never been there during the crest of its high tourist season. The city seemed strained under their weight, and as I boarded a *vaporetto* I could literally feel the boat shudder as it shunted from the dock. I was heading out toward the beach at Lido to lie in the sun, gradually reacquainting myself with the sea-like rhythms of the city—afternoons at the shore ebbing into sunset, evening strolls along canals, wet moonlight lapping against stone.

At least that's what I kept telling myself.

On the third day I had to face the fact I was sleeping past midday, then gorging myself on bread and café latte, then wandering till I could again sleep. This wasn't re-acquaintance or ritual or jet lag. Just my age-old avoidance of what I couldn't face. I'd traveled thousands of miles to visit Alessandro, yet there I was, still backpedaling. That afternoon, I gathered enough courage to dial his family's phone number.

"*Pronto?*"

"*Si, si pronto.* It's me."

"*Ah, finalmente,*" said Aless' sister.

"*Si. Sono arrivato. Sono stato ...*" I started to make an excuse, but she cut me off.

"No, it's good the time. Aless returned yesterday from hospital."

I wondered if this was good or bad news.

"*Si, è a casa,*" she said. "He is home. Now he sleeps, but ..."

I tried to formulate a decent question in my mind. Will he recognize me? Can he see at all? Leave the apartment? All around me young bodies were sunning themselves, running across the beach, eating *gelati*. The telephone clicked and I deposited another coin to keep the call alive.

"*Ma dove sei?*"

"Me? Uh, here, on the street."

"But where do you stay?"

"With another friend. I'm okay. I'm over here ..." I said, then with embarrassment added, "on the Lido."

"*Ah, Lido ...*"

I waited for her to say more, then just blurted out, "Look, can he see me? I mean, can I see him?"

But she didn't respond, her mother at that moment taking hold of the receiver.

"*Vieni da mangiare con noi,*" she said. "*Va bene? Staséra. Vieni e basta.*"

"Okay," I said. "Okay," and hung up.

A meal, I thought. *Una cena*. Good idea. Something to divert the awkwardness, something simple. Yes, I was making this much too complex. Enough with all these questions and preparations. This ongoing evasion. A simple dinner with my friend and his family, that's all.

I went back and sat on the beach. I watched the people along the shoreline. A mother being splashed by her daughter. Long-waisted men. German tourists, Japanese. Grains of sand.

Before the sun began to sink I walked back to the other side of the island toward the public boats. Across the lagoon I could see the outline of Venice's horizon of steeples—focusing on the great curving cupola of the *Salute*, built as a votive to the Virgin for ending the great plague of 1630. Beneath its foundation they'd sunk a million pilings to hold it fast and afloat. Venice, a city knee-deep in miracles. Survivor of catastrophes, flood, contagion. I stopped into a shop and bought a trayful of pastries to bring for dessert, selecting ones I recalled Aless liked. Then I went next door and set the package on the bar. I ordered a wine, then drank a second.

I remember one of the last times I went to visit my father before he died. Finally died, I should say, since he lay in coma for three weeks prior. I remember the evening's weather was raw and raining, and when the commuter train stopped, its doors opened onto a deep grey mist. I could hardly see my hands let alone the platform, and in that moment of taking my next blind step, I admitted to myself he would not survive. I stood

227

immobile on the cement platform for several minutes, the air thick, suffocating. I imagined this is how it might feel to be in a coma. How dying itself might be. The bottom of my lungs balked, the bottoms of my feet. Don't move, I thought. Just don't move and maybe, just maybe--then a rush of wind came, a glowing train speeding by in the opposite direction, and off to my left I glimpsed a stairwell.

Alessandro's family lived on the top floor of an apartment building not far from Venice's bus and train stations. In its courtyard stood an old stone well, covered over centuries ago. I walked past it, rang their bell, and looked up. The last of the sun still shone on the fourth floor, bathing Alessandro's sister orange when she momentarily leaned out the window. A buzzer sounded and the outer door unlocked.

The stairwell beyond the door possessed the same precise quality of grey as that train platform. Its walls and its dust, thick and suffocating. As if all the fading dusk had been sucked toward the upper floors like the last light draining from a room just before the candle expires.

"Is that you?" someone called.

"Yes, yes I'm coming."

I willed my feet forward, climbing flight after flight, growing heavier and breathless with each step. Finally I reached the upper floor, where their apartment door stood ajar. The thought raced through my head that I could still run. I could still--the sound of utensils from within, whispers. I pushed open the door and stepped inside. An umbrella leaned against the foyer wall, a pair of shoes nearby without laces. The smell of oregano. In the kitchen, bowls of minestrone sat steaming on the table beneath upturned faces.

"We waited, but ..."

"Oh no, of course. I'm late. I'm--"

Across the table sat Alessandro, silhouetted before the still bright window. I couldn't see his face, only the outline of his head—the hair much shorter than I remembered, the ears pointed, his neck and shoulders drawn. As I grew accustomed to the light I noticed he wasn't wearing a shirt, that his whole body was listing, his right arm bent at an odd angle. And he was seated in a wheelchair. A yellow wheelchair.

"*Siediti. Siediti,*" said his mother, and placed a bowl before the one empty chair.

I set down my backpack against the wall. Broken bread lay on the table. A bottle of wine. Salt. I sat and inched my chair forward. No one spoke for a full minute, then Alessandro's father pushed a spoon into his son's hand. I watched my friend blindly struggle to find the edge of his soup bowl. After several clinking attempts, he succeeded then awkwardly raised his spoon. The right side of his mouth wouldn't respond, though. Half the liquid ran down his cheek and splashed the tablecloth.

Aless' sister quickly dabbed her napkin to his face, and said, "Look who came to see you, Aless?"

"*Si,*" said his father. "*Il tuo amico Americano.*"

Aless tilted his head to the side like a bird trying to see something before him. I suddenly realized I hadn't gone to embrace him.

4 Agosto. Morning after, and remembering one can again wake howsoever begrudgingly to the vertical. To the living. To soft voices and footsteps outside the shuttered windows. To notice the slice of sun between those shutters and go out and buy a handful of apricots and bread and walk along a street shaded by hanging laundry and cypress, and sit by an open window with a hot cup of espresso. And that there is even music. And yet …

After one visit, gone is much of my anxiety and all my romanticism of a mission here. And what's left? Barely what? A household going through the motions. End time. It seems I am already too late. Oh, he's still alive, but… there's no will left in him. No spark. Beyond blindness, beyond paralysis, a kind of dementia has seeped into his body. Doing only what he is told now. Operating purely on reflexes. To eat, to drink, to bring whatever's placed in his hand to his mouth—the sugar container, the ashtray—to not even realize he is or isn't drinking. I sat there neither able to move nor speak, to be present nor extract myself. I fear my presence only makes things harder for them. The tension in the room, like that moment after dinner, after his father lit a cigarette and placed it in Aless' fist. All our eyes fixed on that silent, dangling ash.

4 Agosto. Evening. Went back today. Forced myself to try again and harder. Sat alone with him in his childhood room for most of the afternoon and it seemed more bearable. The two of us passing time, like brothers. Like he was merely home from school sick and I was keeping him company. The fan banking back and forth against the stifling heat. He kept drifting in and out, but there were tiny moments of awareness today. A sudden frustration when he couldn't remember something. A smile, a genuine response. A shared moment from out of our past. I think that's the hardest part. This mooring of memory. The weight of it, the sheer and sudden beauty of it compared to what now sat in the room. I'm sorry but I can't reconcile the two. Can't accept such decay. I sat and read to him from the lone English book I found on the shelf—"The Little Prince." His one good hand in mine, his palm sweating as he fell asleep, the tattoos on his fingers ...

No, I take it back. The hardest part is coming back out into the world. To recall there is another world going on at the same time—and that I could enter it at will. The sensation for the moment—culpevole. Yes, guilty. I don't think I can go back there again.

5 Agosto. Lido. Out here floating in the Adriatic like a piece of driftwood. The sky a marble of blue and cloud veins. Is this how it will be—to die to float, to release to currents? To know no difference between sea and sky? To lose your body? I flashed on an image of my own brother, pictured him gasping in his tiny oxygen tent. This fear in me, full-fathomed.

6 Agosto. Okay, enough·of this self-bemoaning. Sure you're tired, you're sapped, but what about Aless? What about his fears, his exhaustion? Imagine what he can and can't stop thinking ... Fine, so you'll make your little trip. You'll come and give your little handshakes and hugs, your little comforts ... and then you'll leave. Leave them to sweep up the mess. To collect the piss pots and soiled sheets and tears and, eventually, the body. Leave them the weight of having to call you with the ultimate news. That awkward, utter silence. You'll pack and go back to your little life, having saved nothing, changed nothing. Risked nothing but the price of plane fare ... All you wanted

to discuss, to bridge, your so-called closure—all too late. You comfort
only yourself, and cheaply.

There are over one hundred and forty bridges in Venice—and most of them, no matter how small, with their own popular names and yarns. Amidst the maze of islands and alleyways that comprise the city these bridges are your only hope of getting anywhere. Traversing Venice is in many ways like tracking in the woods—always a matter of taking note of the signs between one place and another. Always having to reorient yourself.

Yet the bridges of Venice span not only space, but time as well. Touch their railings or worn steps and you are tracing ages of iron, of wood, of stone. But don't be too sure of yourself, of that which you're touching being solid, of history. For Venice above all is not about bridges but about water, and water is a dream, a forever shifting illusion. In truth there's no real land in Venice, only pilings. There's nowhere to get to either, at least not in any hurry. Venice confounds us with how we often move in our lives—setting out with clear goals or destinations, then finding we've somehow circled back to where we began. There are no straight streets or canals in Venice. Like rivers they meander because that is the path of least resistance. The path I'd chosen my whole life.

And returning to Venice was churning up all the stagnant waters and uncrossed bridges of my past. I was staying at the same apartment in San Rocco where I'd once rented out a room. Its back window overlooked an adjoining yard belonging to the

Frari, one of Venice's two major monastic churches. I recalled how each morning I used to open my window shutters and listen to the bells calling mass, then watch the church gardener rake his rows of radicchio and fennel. He had this dog too, a German shepherd, who always trailed right behind him.

One morning, the friend who rented me the room came in to retrieve her hanging laundry.

"Good morning," she'd said, stretching out over the window sill.

"*Giorno.*"

"It is beautiful morning, no?"

"*Si, una bella giornata.*"

We traded each other's languages, part of our rental agreement.

"How do you say *il contadino*?"

"Farmer," I said, "but in this case you'd probably say gardener."

"Ah, yes," she said. "You watch the gardener?"

"Are you watching the gardener? *Si, lo guardo.*"

"It is fascinating, no, how he works with one arm?"

"*Cosa?*"

"With one arm. You see? He has one arm only."

I looked down and noticed the way the rake handle was wedged under one shoulder, the gardener's opposite arm hanging limp at his side. I suddenly realized why he always leaned his tools against his chest to toss a ball to his dog, or to wave to me. My friend gathered the last of her sheets and clothespins.

"It is better for you to close the windows, is very humid today … You come take a *café*?"

"Huh? Oh yes, yes," I said, but did not move.

I heard her slippers shuffle away behind me, cupboards opening and closing in the kitchen. The gardener moved toward the far end of the yard to check his grapevines. I noted the slight slant to his left shoulder as he walked, the frozen fingers of his prosthesis pointing to the earth. For months I had watched him. For months.

Then I recalled another instance, months later, when I again lingered before this same window. It was New Year's Eve and I stood watching the garden's stucco walls quietly change colors with the sinking sun. A monk was pacing the circumference of the yard with his arms clasped behind his brown robe. The gardener was there too, leaning against an open back door to the church, his loyal dog sitting nearby. Soon it would be dark, a night I would typically have been sharing with Sybil. Sharing our traditional dinner and theater, then the midnight fireworks in Central Park. Then the whole long night together, nestled in each other's arms. That is, if I wasn't across the ocean.

And I remembered that afternoon as the precise moment I first recognized I might have come to Venice to leave Sybil. And now, years later, here I was again, back in Venice and still frozen in fear before that same window. Still denying the fact I *had* left Sybil, back then in Italy and now again in Iowa. And that's what this glacial paralysis of mine was really about—not only that I'd have to leave her, but that I'd have to be the one to end it. *That's* what I couldn't seem to face—that I'd have to both initiate and be accountable for that loss.

Sybil had once intimated so much herself—saying she'd be willing to stay with me as long as I'd have her. I recalled how those words leaked out almost in passing, as if she were thinking aloud. Among the bubble of our myopic day-to-days she'd admitted at least that much to herself. She could foresee at least that much of the future to want to forestall it. Me, I was still far too naïve to have grasped such an awareness, let alone openly address it. Hell, I was *still* in a fog about what letting go of Sybil might bring.

There are all kinds of amputations and oversights in this world. All kinds of cripples. At some point in the past that gardener must have been careless, inattentive. Just as Alessandro had been in that moment he shared a needle. Just as I was being careless by way of remaining too careful. Careful in friendships, love, confrontations, you name it. Always keeping my measured distance, or else running away, staving off not only loss, but life in the process.

Meanwhile, outside the window there was no longer any gardener or dog and the Frari's courtyard lay long overgrown with weeds. And Sybil, she was still across the ocean. Still, in my mind, shielded by distance and silence. By my not ending us. Yet in truth, I wasn't protecting her. Never had, just myself. No wonder she was angry. I'd been doling out the very hurt and unkindness we'd so hoped to avoid. Prolonging her pain, in fact. That's not what I'd ever wanted to do. Surely not what she deserved. So crippled or not, it was time for me to step up, to bridge distances and decency. Starting right here and now. And right here and now, I had another loved one nearby who truly was paralyzed and lying in a bed facing the ultimate loss, and each and every moment the tide was turning. My chance was now. My choices at hand, just as they'd always been.

7 Agosto. Near midnight. Spent the evening with Alessandro and his family. Today, his birthday. Thirty-five. His mother cooked all his favorites: risi e bisi, sarde in saor, peoci—a true fish fest. Aless' brother was there too, all upbeat and joking. Made me wonder if this is how I should have been for the rest of them too, how I could have been reacting. And yet...Every day Aless loses something: a word, a phrase, the capacity to blow his nose. And today? The chance for another birthday. Looking across the table at Aless' real brother, I saw he'd soon be a brother left behind, too. The two of us, brothers in loss. And it occurred to me that in a way Aless HAD become the older brother I never had. The brother I would once again never have.

8 Agosto. Worse today. He kept falling forward in the wheelchair. Trouble drinking, too. He'd breathe in, causing hiccups. And so self-disgusted today, apologizing when wheeled back from the bathroom. I found myself losing it at the kitchen table. His sister, too. The nurse came this afternoon with more shots, his arm already a pincushion of bruises. Usually I'm okay once I get inside the apartment, but couldn't seem to bear it today. That smell of ammonia. That sad, half smile of his. His paralysis hideous, mocking. I can't do this. I can't do this...

Despite my best intentions, the next day I retreated under the guise of visiting another local friend. *Rico delle Scimmie*, or Rico of the Monkeys, as he was called, since he lived with over twenty of them in a remote working class section of Venice. The first few he'd fished out of the port where he used to work as a stevedore—tossed overboard by sailors who'd bought them on a lark in Macau. Others came from the mainland via society folk who'd grown bored with an outmoded pet, and still others from those monkeys who'd managed to breed under his care. Fourth generation in the case of his vervets. Rico's home also hosted a hundred or so exotic birds, a few turtles, dogs, dozens of cats. At one time he had a goat as well, and usually a broken seagull or two he'd nurse back to health before releasing. Neighbors often knocked at his door seeking advice for a sick pet, sometimes even a sick child.

For over sixty years Rico had lived in the same three-story house in which he was born and had since adapted with a whole system of cages and runways to allow his monkeys easy access and egress. However, about a year after I'd last left Venice, he was forced out by real estate speculators citing a hygiene technicality. Under much duress, Rico relocated his menagerie to a stone house and some rustic acreage on the mainland.

I arrived at his tiny village's train depot late morning and walked the last couple of kilometers to his remote house. We greeted each other then spent much of the afternoon transplanting young fruit trees and feeding the animals. This was how he and I usually passed our time together—sharing more work than words. Rico spoke only a thick Venetian dialect, much of which still eluded me. Plus, by now he'd lost even more of his teeth. With his dated eyeglasses, he looked a little like Woody Allen in both stature and expression, though with a bushy silver beard. As well, a frayed red turban held down his wiry mop of hair, a souvenir from his time in North Africa during World War II.

As I was helping Rico repair a section of roofing over his balcony that afternoon, I reached down to grab a hammer from him and recalled how I used to accompany my father on service calls—helping him fix customers' TV antennas up on their roofs. While I never considered taking after my father's trade, the idea of following in Rico's footsteps had more than once crossed my mind in the past. As it turned out, his life as a recluse and mine at the schoolhouse weren't all that different. We were both living lives of avoidance and exile.

Toward dusk we went indoors to feed ourselves. Meals with Rico were always simple—food plucked from the same crates and stovetop that fed his animals. Rico ate with fingers half bent, like the monkeys themselves. We spoke about Redbird's acreage in Iowa, and he seemed most impressed by its many ponds and two creeks. I'd wondered if he missed Venice and her canals.

"Have you been back?" I asked.

"Once. Twice," he said.

I tried to push further, but Rico was never interested in talking about the past. Or about himself, for that matter. He wasn't living apart and surrounding himself with the injured for nothing. Maybe that's why I could relate to him so much. We were both drawn to broken birds. Both were broken birds.

I watched him reach for a cooked potato. He split it into quarters then sprinkled on lemon and pepper. Near the old stove sat a huge twenty-seven-inch television he constantly left playing for a voice. A soccer match was droning. I got hold of the remote control and found the mute switch.

"Rico," I said, "have you ever been in love?"

"Me? No... Once, maybe. I was seventeen."

"And ..."

"Nothing. The girl wanted to marry, make a mama. It wasn't my choice."

On his lap sat one monkey, gently grooming and picking at Rico's beard.

"And never again?"

"No."

The kitchen door started to rattle, another monkey named Gina trying to get in. Rico cursed at her. Actually, worse. In Italy you could curse or you could blaspheme—cursing with risk. Evidently Gina knew the difference, because the rattling stopped. Rico went back to eating. All in all, he seemed calmer out here in the country, further still from people.

"And have you ever been afraid?" I asked.

Rico patiently swallowed a handful of fruit, then said, "No... Not much. Not even when they were bombing."

I'd heard of his war stories—about a tour he did in Tunisia, and of the mistaken American bombing of nearby Treviso, the sky over Venice black with planes. I also knew he'd later worked side by side with Alessandro's father at the port. With Alessandro.

"But loss? What about loss?"

"Ooh, I saw many dead during the war. The first one to have to carry them was always me."

"But now I mean, do you think of death now?"

"No. I'm not ready."

He said this so matter-of-factly, I had to laugh.

"But if I ever do feel something, I say ai."

"Ai?"

"Yes. Ai!!! And it goes away."

On the television, soccer players ran across the pitch. Some were dressed in red, some in yellow. I could hear rustling parakeets through the wall and a distant train's moan, a cat tipping over pans on the porch. All the collective noises we made in the dark.

I thought about Rico and all his animals. I knew he worried deeply about them, and that over the years his commitment and care had become its own breed of intimacy. And yet I knew it could never be mutual. At the end of the day he was living out here alone and apart, listening for faint human voices on his television. Was this the kind of existence I was heading toward? What I'd really want to choose?

Not all too far from Rico's lay the small town of Noale—quiet and unassuming, with an old castle dating from medieval times. Once, when Sybil came to visit me in Venice, we took a bus out there despite the threat of rain. I recall our strolling among its stone clock tower and green gardens, and this pair of white swans floating on a pond beneath the drizzle. There was a cemetery nearby, small and colorful like most cemeteries in the Veneto. The photograph I took of Sybil that day, however, is black and white—half-shielded beneath her umbrella, her linen jacket hanging open, her glance off to the side. And in the background, rows of tombstones, each bearing its own tiny porcelain photograph of the deceased.

I knew this photograph by heart, perhaps my favorite of her among the bookshelf stack waiting for me back at the schoolhouse in Iowa. Enshrined in its worn envelope.

I glanced back at Rico, the monkey still on his lap.

"But Rico," I said. "What do you think happens after we die?"

"Ah, the big question," he said, pausing to feed the monkey a wedge of fruit. "If you ask me, when you lose your senses you no longer exist. Heaven, Hell? What the priests tell you? I don't believe it, not in the least what they say."

He reached for another clementine and broke its skin.

"However, I'm convinced that if they place you in the ground there'll be worms born. Little worms, without eyes or legs. Who knows what kind of life they lead, underground the way they do. You see them, you don't see them. There are machines that can sense such things, but I don't know...but I am certain that once you're inside such a worm, one day a bird will come to eat you then shit you back down to the ground to fertilize the trees. Or else carry you back to a nest and feed her young so that one day you too can fly. Either way, you join all the rest. The animals, the trees, the air, the water...this is another thought, bigger than death."

One night while my father lay in coma—and as it turned out, his last night—I took photographs of him. Something about the act seemed obscene to me even as I was doing it, yet I continued, literally leaning over his bed to adjust the covers then backing myself into the corner of the room to compose the images. It was a roll of slide film I shot, which about a week after the funeral I received in the mail in a small, square box. I never opened that box, no doubt too afraid to face what hid inside, yet those slides still lay in some old shoebox in my mother's basement, nestled among the childhood photographs of me and the mimosa on those first days of elementary school.

I remember how each year the teacher would scratch the words "What I Did On My Summer Vacation" onto the blackboard then promptly hand out construction paper. There would always be colorful pictures drawn, filled with station wagons and swimming pools, watermelons, flowers. And as we grew older, those crayons turned into No. 2 pencils and ballpoints, into penmanship and essays, "remembrances of things past."

Thinking about all the novels and novellas set in Venice, what I envision above all else is a theme of morbidity. Stories plagued by decadence or the macabre or, at the very least, intrigue. Certainly a sadness. Regrets. The colors mostly white on white, blacks, greys. Maybe a deep red here or there. A midnight blue. Meanwhile, the painters of Venice, who must carry similar doubts and longings, can't deny themselves a wider palette. Their garret studios, howsoever remote, must let in light and its prism of colors. They cannot enclose themselves or their work within. At worst, there is chiaroscuro.

In one form or another, I've spent years writing about my father, or by extension, my brother. And now, Sybil. About all that went unspoken, unbridged. All that has remained in the dark. To some extent all writing is about the past. All writing, a shrine. Painters also record, and yet ... I would never think of trying to paint a portrait of that grey stairwell. Never. I should have been a painter.

11 Agosto. Aless seemed a little better today. Moments of clarity. Presence. Noticed his long-term memory seems more intact. And in effect, this is what we have to share now, more past than present. Only a couple more days left till I leave. Now wishing there was more time. We're still only halfway through "The Little Prince."

12 Agosto. He was sleeping when I visited this morning, so I just sat beside the bed. Started sketching his body—the lost tone, the dead right arm ... the old schoolbooks and wooden pull toys on a near shelf, the boxes of medicine on the night table ... the wheelchair, whose hue of yellow, I noted, matched the Little Prince's blond hair on the book cover. Matched that tiny sunburst candy wrapper back on Lexington Avenue... "'What is essential is invisible to the eye,' the Little Prince repeated, so that he would be sure to remember."

Later on, stood beside Aless' mother at the kitchen window, handing her clothespins. One by one I watched her attach Aless' laundered sheets to the line and release them to the wind. Beyond, ceramic rooftops and steeples. I wondered if she knew Alessandro wanted to be cremated and have his ashes spread in the lagoon. Out onto the water...

Which reminds me. Right before I left for Venice, Beth called to wish me a good trip and to remind me to try and stay open to whatever I was feeling. She also shared something she'd heard around the time her father died. Something she'd never forgotten. How death was like dropping a pebble in a lake. Of course those closest to the rock would feel the most waves while those furthest might not even sense a ripple, yet the entire lake would be slightly displaced. Changed, risen... And then, before hanging up, she told me not to forget to also enjoy the view.

On the last afternoon of my trip, I took a ferry out past the Lido where the string of littorals protecting the Venetian lagoon gradually thinned, and the shoreline became a great jetty of stone boulders buttressing three tiny fishing villages from the sea. Among these random rocks rested huge trunks of driftwood, long beached and bleached by the waves. And at my feet, varied other trinkets the sea had left behind: bits of old wooden crates and cork buoys, strands of fishing nets, washed up medicine vials, sea glass, and shells. I fell asleep on one of those warm rocks and when I awoke the sun had moved and the tide receded. Hours had passed me by, the day already dimming. The near waves were the color of bruises, yet out in the distance floated a boat. Its sails a shimmer of white, appearing and disappearing among the crests and troughs. So remote. Intangible.

Still, it struck me that despite the distance there was a bridge between the boat and my eye. And even if it were to drift out beyond sight, I still knew it was there just as the boat would still be connected to the shoreline, for there is no being at sea without a shore. In a way there is no amputation then, I thought. Memory, not only a shipwreck, but a harbor to return to again and again. Like a photograph, a shoebox. A meal all wrapped up and waiting inside a freezer. A shelved heart waiting to beat anew. There is no loss without gain, I thought. Maybe there is no loss then, only gain.

I sat on the shore's edge and watched that distant boat among the waves. Both its comings and its goings struck me as equally beautiful to witness, and one no less natural than the other... and each of them a gift. I'd gotten this all wrong, I realized. In the end this trip wasn't about death. It was about love. I wasn't losing Alessandro or Sybil, I'd gained them.

I gathered my belongings from among the rocks and walked toward the nearest village, whose cobbled streets lay quiet and whose fishing boats gently rocked in their moorings. Dusk was descending and to the west Venice's lagoon played its age-old trick of light. I'd seen it many times before, the water's surface glowing both green and rust, a phosphorescent dance of cellophane and eternity.

Soon the evening sky offered up its constellations. Night fell and in the nearer distance tiny lights were turning on one by one all over Venice, too. The jewel of the Adriatic igniting her palaces and bell towers, her stone white bridges. Her Bridge of Sighs. And standing there, I swear I felt something rise up out of my chest. Something that broke free and let go. Call it a weight. A waiting. Whatever. One thing for sure, my next breath felt deeper than I'd ever remembered.

The following morning I packed my bags for the train station and spent my last half hour in Venice at Alessandro's bedside. He was more himself, more conscious than at any other time during my visit. This was good, yet had its disadvantages as well. He was more aware of his condition and its weight. Aware that I was there and that I'd be leaving.

He asked me to help place him in his wheelchair so I could see him sitting upright. Carefully I slid him off the bed, and stepping back noticed he was wincing.

"What's wrong?" I asked.

He struggled to swallow and clutched at the arm of the wheelchair. I could see his shoulders quivering against the pain. When the shaking finally subsided, he raised his head and whispered, "I'm so afraid."

I wanted to scream. Scream every goddamn blasphemy I'd ever heard, scream so fucking loud that time itself would stop.

I wanted to run. I wanted to hide. I wanted to hold him in my arms and somehow explain everything I'd felt out on the rocky shore. About the sailboat and the tides and the dusk and the stars. I wanted to make my words all add up to that glowing moment at the water's edge, but when the words came all I managed was, "Yes. I know, Aless. I am, too." It seemed the most honest words I could say.

I knelt before the yellow wheelchair and took his hands in mine, first the good one and then the bad. On his fingers were little tattoos—a small round dot in the crevice between one thumb and forefinger, two on a pinkie, six in all. I knew each mark represented a specific old friend, each of whom shared a corresponding mark on their own hands. For the last year or so I'd wanted to ask him if we could do the same, but was always too afraid. I rubbed the little constellations on his fingers.

"You know, I've been thinking about getting a tattoo," I said. "For us."

Aless looked toward me, though his eyes could not see.

"Here," I said, and pressed three of his fingers against the place on my wrist where I'd mapped out the space. "Three dots right here. What do you think?"

Alessandro's fingers slid from my wrist to my palm and pressed of their own will.

"You don't need for to do this," he said, "mark yourself for me."

"No, but I want to."

I wished I could explain my reasons. How they weren't about making a shrine to the past anymore, but to celebrate it. Celebrate what was still in that room between us.

"I want to," I repeated. "I will, when I get back to the States."

Aless pulled back his good hand and lay it in his lap.

"You have to go now, no?" he said.

Outside the window several pigeons reeled in flight. I heard others steadily cooing from the near rooftops.

"Yes, the train's leaving soon."

In my mind I could see it already waiting at the station. Could see it pulling away, like that tiny white boat out in the waves. I looked at Alessandro, a mere foot or two between us. I looked very carefully at his face and beautiful blind eyes, right there in front of me, right now. And in my mind, I took a photograph. Then I lunged forward and embraced him. I held him long and I held him close.

"Thank you," he said, "for coming."

Thank me, I thought, thank me? I could feel the breathing in his chest. His words, pushing out.

"You have to go now," he said. "Please, go."

I didn't want to, but peeled myself away. I walked across the room, and reached for my bags.

"Why three," he asked. "Three dots?"

I turned and stood there a moment, choosing my words.

"One for you. And one for me," I said. "And one for what will always remain between us."

"Oh," he said nodding, then a moment later smiled and added, "Be careful of the needle."

Joseph Brodsky has written that to leave Venice always feels as if you are leaving it forever. "For leaving is a banishment of the eye... And to the eye, for purely optical reasons, departure is not the body leaving the city but the city abandoning the pupil... A tear is the anticipation of the eye's future."

I stumbled down that grey staircase and out onto the streets. Stumbled forward, toward the train station.

Commencement

16 August. Somewhere over the Atlantic. Somewhere between departing and arriving. But not circling. No, I don't feel like I'm floating or hovering anymore...Down below I can see tiny waves in motion. Rivers, rain, tears... they only flow in one direction...

More snippets of wisdom from "The Little Prince:"

> *It is the time you have wasted for your rose that makes your rose so important... You become responsible, forever, for what you have tamed. You are responsible for your rose ...*

"I am responsible for my rose," the little prince repeated, so that he would be sure to remember.

I sat in the plane with my journal and *The Little Prince* beside me, and the tiny waves down below. From such a height it didn't seem so hard to regard the world as a place that both ebbed and flowed, a place with as much potential ahead as there was past behind. Like my grandmother, the one who plucked chickens, used to say, "Every closed door has an open window." It just took me years to learn such changes don't merely happen of their own accord.

As we neared the shores of America, I thought about that grandmother and her initial voyage west from the old country. She'd made her crossing of the Atlantic in steerage, down among these same churning waves. Surely she must have been harboring doubts over leaving her loved ones behind, the family and old friends she'd presumably never see again. I thought about all of my family—the butcher and the blind, the hungry and the hanged, the haunted, the hopeful. The fathers and the sons, the mothers, the daughters. I thought of all of us the world over, each and every one immigrants of a sort. Each thrust from some warm, safe womb out onto this foreign shore, yet within moments adapting to its sudden light and chill. Within moments, stretching out tiny fingers for what lay next. And, above all, for contact.

At first sight of land I thought of Sybil too, somewhere down there in New York City. And this time, I didn't recoil.

I knew I needed to contact her now, to reach out and maybe even visit face-to-face, one last time. I needed to finally embrace that responsibility of resolution. Perhaps we could meet near that spot on Lexington Avenue and ... No, who was I kidding? That moment had long since passed us by. At best, we'd choose a neutral location to meet, somewhere neither colored nor confused with our past. And chances are it would be anything but cinematic. No flutter of snowflakes over our heads along the avenue. No lilting soundtrack fading into a perfectly scripted dialogue in which all would be admitted and forgiven. All happily-ever-after. Roll credits.

No, it wouldn't be any fictional finale. It would be as awkward and rending and real as my returning to Venice. But I'd go just the same, and offer her the decency she so deserved, the dignity. First and foremost, I'd need to apologize for my weaknesses of character. For whatever hurt I may have caused. Somehow I'd let my fears overwhelm all our other pleasures and pains, all the many lessons on beauty and drama and story I'd learned at her side. Let it overshadow our love, which above all was what should endure between us. That undeniable gift we'd shared for however long we could. That gain.

And of course she'd have the chance to say her fill too—whatever that might be—and I'd listen carefully and then we'd talk, and ... No wait, this too was wholly absurd of me to still presume. Perhaps she would refuse to meet. Perhaps she couldn't forgive me any longer, or by now had gotten beyond this on her own. Who knew? One thing for sure though—I needed to make that initial contact to at least offer her the choice. To allow us at least the chance to finally celebrate as well as release one another. And the sooner, the better.

On this day, however, the plane did not land in New York. It continued on toward the Middle West and that other unexpected hearth I'd found named Iowa. And as its fertile shores slowly came into view and the plane began to drop, I sensed not a queasiness, but a settled feeling inside. A sense I could steward my life after all.

At the airport gate Beth was waiting for me, which felt lovely and lucky. She stood there smiling and I didn't hesitate to embrace her. She also offered to help carry my baggage, and I let her. Inside was packed a little gift I'd bought for her. I hoped she'd like it. We exited to the parking lot and it felt good to speak in English again and, above all, to hear her voice. To be sharing words, and feelings. Her hair seemed longer than I remembered. Redder. A color I realized I really liked now.

As she drove me home I noted the crops were showing signs of drying out from the flood, the corn recovering. I kept glancing over at Beth too, there beside me in the car. Again, I felt so damn lucky. Being alone and apart wasn't all it was cracked up to be after all.

Heading back from the airport, we took a different route than Black Diamond Road, and as the last dirt road crested and in the offing we spotted the schoolhouse, Beth rolled us to a stop. It looked different from this northerly approach—rather small in relation to its surrounding hillside and trees. A tiny brown box half-wrapped in ivy. Looking as if it could fit in the palm of my hand. My pocket.

On the plane, I'd also been thinking about what Frank Conroy had drawn on the blackboard back on our very first night of class. That rainbow-shaped arc with the Reader at one end and the Writer at the other. And he was right, one should aspire toward the crest of the arc, midway between so the exchange could be a co-creation. Yet by now I'd also learned I needed not only focus my efforts toward one point on the arc, but on the overall arc itself. That my greater task, both on and off the page, was to reach out and make a personal connection with whomever was at the receiving end of that arc. That to bridge distances and touch someone else was what mattered most. In my words and deeds.

Someone, though I can't remember whom, once told me that School and Life were different; in school they give you the lessons before the test, in life it's the other way around.

I reached for Beth's idling hand, and together we shifted the car into gear.

The air inside the schoolhouse smelled musty. Beth helped me open all the windows then went to make us coffee. I gazed out at the wide horizon, whose panorama more or less matched the topmost strip of photographs hanging on the adjacent wall. I'd snapped its image precisely a year ago. Nothing more to record there, I thought. In fact, there were many things on the surrounding walls—feathers, skulls, pelts, thistles—that seemed strangely dated. Odd keepsakes I now needed to return to their rightful places in the woods.

I stepped outside onto the deck, its railings once again wrapped in burdock and flowering jewelweed. The ivied walls of the schoolhouse were starting to blush and at the edge of the woods I could see blackberries once again coloring the brambles. I'll head out a little later, I thought.

Coming up the drive was Tina, with her shock of silvered hair and strident step. She was wearing a dress, a bright print. In her hands was a pile of my mail. Half were probably bills, some hopefully letters from friends.

"So," she said, "a good voyage?"

"Yes," I said, meeting her eyes. "Good to have gone. Good to come home."

"Good, I hoped so." She glanced about at the hillside, then handed me my mail. "Well, do come down for tea later this afternoon and we can talk. If you'd like, that is."

"Yes, yes I would … May I bring Beth?"

Tina smiled, waving at a window behind me. "That'd be nice. I'd like that, very much." Then she turned and started heading back downhill.

"Aren't you going for your woodswalk?" I called.

"No," she said, "I only came up to give you your mail. But watch where you're walking later. The oaks are already dropping their acorns. More than usual, in response to the flood."

❧

Thoreau once said the earth itself was both granary and seminary, and though he did not believe a plant would spring up where no seed had fallen, he still had great faith in a seed. Growth and change, after all, are the natural order. Individuals, species, ecosystems all evolve, eventually. We grow into what we are, what we'll become. Yet Thoreau also wrote, "A man receives only what he is ready to receive, whether physically or intellectually or morally... We hear and apprehend only what we already half know.... Every man thus tracks *himself* through life, in all his hearing and reading and observation and traveling."

I sat on the schoolhouse deck and pulled over my backpack. I cracked open my journal and duly wrote down the date, but then set the pen aside, preferring to simply breathe in the surrounding air and colors and moment. From inside the schoolhouse, I could hear cupboards opening and closing, the tinkling of utensils and plates. Beth and I were going to cook ourselves a special lunch to celebrate my year's anniversary at the schoolhouse, which I'd missed while in Italy. In all probability, it would be both my first and last. But that was okay. I held the schoolhouse within me already. And there'd be other homes to gain, perhaps one Beth and I could create together. Perhaps even a child we could raise to carry that love forward.

As I was getting up to go help her, a cloud burst overhead. The sudden downpour caught me unaware, yet instead of running for shelter I stayed put on the deck. I stripped off all my clothes and let the rain wash over me. Through the screen windows I could hear Beth's laughter, and waved for her to come join me. Meanwhile, I hopped over the railing and started somersaulting down the hillside. Behind me my journal sat open on the tabletop, its ink running off the page, down through the slats of the schoolhouse deck, back down into the earth.

• • •

Acknowledgments

❦

Given the rendering of this book has spanned some two decades, there are many many people to thank. I'll start by asking forgiveness of those I'll inevitably omit. If you don't locate your name below, know it's warmly tucked away in my chest.

Firstly, thanks to my steadfast and patient readers. The older guard: J.C. Hallman, Marina Harris, Darleen Lev, Edward Radtke, Lisa Schlesinger, Jo Tavener, Whitney Terrell, Rick Zollo. And the newer generation: Laura Castonguay, Alex Friedman, Jolene McIlwain, Lynda Schuster, Phil Terman. And to those who listened to its very first iterations around the campfire: Pete Hendley, Jim Levi, and Fred Redekop.

Thanks to those heady Iowa classrooms and fellow classmates, glowing among the tutelage of Ethan Canin, Robert Cohen, Frank Conroy, Paul Diehl, Deborah Eisenberg, Margot Livesey, James Alan McPherson, Marilynne Robinson, Tom Simmons. And a special shout out to the Iowa Summer Writing Festival, who offered me that first seat at a round table, and Wayne Johnson who pointed the way. And Chris Offutt, Mitchell Moss for enabling my very residence at Redbird.

Thank you other havens of solitude and focus over the years: The Anderson Center for Interdisciplinary Arts, Centrum, Willard R. Espy Literary Foundation, Blacklock Nature Sanctuary, and Unsmoke Systems Artspace. And thanks to the foundations who generously supported my early writing practice: Jerome Foundation, McKnight Foundation, Minnesota State Arts Board.

My ongoing gratitude to those teaching institutions who've also become patrons, allowing me to work on craft while endeavoring to pass it forward: University of Iowa and the Iowa Summer Writing Festival, University of Minnesota and The Loft, University of Pittsburgh and, especially, Chatham University; to all their treasured staffs and colleagues in the hallways.

Thanks, too, to those journals and anthologies who've published excerpts, and to the following editors in particular: Matthew Bohn, Xavier Cavazos, Walter Cummins, Jill and Philip Gerard, David Hamilton, Noelle Havens, Ginny Levy, Carrie Muehle, Lance M. Sacknoff, Tyrone Shaw, Stefanie Brook Trout, Jacob White. My deepest editorial gratitude goes out to Steven Semken, a true one-man band of publication and that rarest of birds one glimpses out in the field perhaps only once in a lifetime. His Ice Cube Press arose before me one morning in all its quiet splendor—the perfect heron, home, and hearth I'd always been waiting to find. Thanks to Adam Jaschen for all his honest and eager efforts. And to Jane Farthing, for her eye, her design, her heart.

My everlasting appreciation to the extended Bourjaily family, and especially Tina, who trusted me to share her land, her legacy, and, I hope, her integrity.

Thanks to all those included in the unfurling of this book's tale. Each and every one of you offered lessons I've come to imbibe, howsoever slowly.

And thanks, finally, to my family—those behind, beside, and moving forward—the one I luckily inherited, and those I've been graced with along the trail. To Beth, for ultimately saving me from myself, and for continuing to share our "oval of possibility." And to Gigi, for your magic self; may your path lead to ever new landscapes and horizons, to enduring love.

The Ice Cube Press began publishing in 1993 to focus on how to live with the natural world and to better understand how people can best live together in the communities they share and inhabit. Using the literary arts to explore life and experiences in the heartland of the United States we have been recognized by a number of well-known writers including: Gary Snyder, Gene Logsdon, Wes Jackson, Patricia Hampl, Greg Brown, Jim Harrison, Annie Dillard, Ken Burns, Roz Chast, Jane Hamilton, Daniel Menaker, Kathleen Norris, Janisse Ray, Craig Lesley, Alison Deming, Harriet Lerner, Richard Lynn Stegner, Rhodes, Michael Pollan, David Abram, David Orr, and Barry Lopez. We've published a number of well-known authors including: Mary Swander, Jim Heynen, Mary Pipher, Bill Holm, Connie Mutel, John T. Price, Carol Bly, Marvin Bell, Debra Marquart, Ted Kooser, Stephanie Mills, Bill McKibben, Craig Lesley, Elizabeth McCracken, Derrick Jensen, Dean Bakopoulos, Rick Bass, Linda Hogan, Pam Houston, and Paul Gruchow. Check out Ice Cube Press books on our web site, join our email list, facebook group, or follow us on twitter. Visit booksellers, museum shops, or any place you can find good books and support true honest to goodness independent publishing so you can discover why we continue striving to, "hear the other side."

Ice Cube Press, LLC (est. 1993)
205 N. Front Street
North Liberty, Iowa 52317-9302
steve@icecubepress.com
twitter @icecubepress
www.icecubepress.com

to Laura Lee & Fenna Marie
finding their ways through
all forms of love and landscape

ENVIRONMENTAL BENEFITS STATEMENT

Ice Cube Press saved the following resources by printing the pages of this book on chlorine free paper made with 100% post-consumer waste.

TREES	WATER	ENERGY	SOLID WASTE	GREENHOUSE GASES
9 FULLY GROWN	**4,005** GALLONS	**4** MILLION BTUs	**268** POUNDS	**739** POUNDS

Environmental impact estimates were made using the Environmental Paper Network Paper Calculator 3.2. For more information visit www.papercalculator.org.